Literacy and ICT
• in the •
Primary School

A Creative Approach to English

Andrew Rudd • Alison Tyldesley

 David Fulton Publishers

David Fulton Publishers Ltd
The Chiswick Centre, 414 Chiswick High Road, London W4 5TF

www.fultonpublishers.co.uk

David Fulton Publishers is a division of Granada Learning Limited, part of ITV plc.

First published in Great Britain in 2006 by David Fulton Publishers

10 9 8 7 6 5 4 3 2 1

Note: The right of the individual contributors to be identified as the authors of their work has been asserted by them in accordance with the Copyright, Designs and Patents Act 1988.

Copyright © Andrew Rudd and Alison Tyldesley 2006

British Library Cataloguing in Publication Data
A catalogue record for this book is available from the British Library.

ISBN 1-84312-374-6

Typeset by FiSH Books, Enfield, Middx
Printed and bound in Great Britain

Contents

Also available:

Science and ICT in the Primary School
A Creative Approach to Big Ideas
John Meadows
1-84312-120-4

Maths and ICT in the Primary School
A Creative Approach
Richard English
1-84312-377-0

Introduction: new literacies and new technologies

A new world of information

The world of communication, literacy and education is changing. In the book-centred culture of a century ago, to 'read' the classics was often considered to be the best education. Good handwriting and the ability to compose formal letters were essential life skills. Throughout the twentieth century a series of major technological changes – telephone, radio, television, computers – has radically redrawn the map of communication. Children growing up in modern Europe socialise and communicate electronically: they are in constant electronic contact with each other through voice, text, pictures and even video. Their primary day-to-day experience of 'reading' comes to them through screens – television, computer, games device or film. The internet allows them to treat a world of information with the casual lightness and inattention of a daydream. Ilana Snyder describes this as a new 'communication order':

> Now, for the first time in history, the written, oral and audiovisual modalities of communication are integrated into the same electronic system – multimodal hypertext systems made accessible via the Internet and the World Wide Web. Being literate in the context of these technologies is to do with understanding how the different modalities are combined in complex ways to create meaning.
>
> (Snyder 2003: 264)

As educators, we have no choice about inhabiting this technological environment – it is very much with us and is highly unlikely to go away. The only choice we have is whether or not to engage in our teaching with these new literacies: and, if so, how to lead children into a mature and independent literacy of their own.

Consider these facts:

We live in a society defined by the production and flow of information on an unprecedented scale. As I write this, Google claims to be able to search 8,058,044,651 web pages – an alarmingly enormous and precise figure. Searching for the exact phrase 'information literacy' brings over a million references. How do

we cope with this deluge of information? Growing up in the twenty-first century obviously requires children and students to be able to handle and communicate information – to access the information they need in a literate way. In this context ICT and literacy together have become more and more important in the curriculum – especially where the learner comes into contact with new and evolving literacies.

New skills

Literacy is no longer limited to reading printed books and other paper texts, but a number of key skills are needed more than ever. Many of these are the traditional skills of reading, scanning, skimming which remain essential in any text-based media. Some new media reading skills appear to be novel and specific, and the teacher of literacy needs to take them into account. Here are several skills which are common to ICT and English. Each one raises important questions which will be explored in more detail in later chapters of this book.

The ability to find information

The reader needs to understand something about the structure of a text in order to navigate a way through it. Books have indexes, tables of contents, page numbers. They are organised in hierarchical and familiar ways which are taught in the literacy hour as a matter of course. What strategies are available to navigate electronic texts and the internet? Where are the signposts and clues? The skills of scanning and skimming are useful in gathering information from books – how are they applicable in the high speed world of electronic communication? Do we as teachers have the knowledge and skills to use search engines effectively to return manageable and relevant lists of data? How can we teach these skills to children? How can we interpret content, skills and progression in this information literacy?

The ability to develop critical thinking and evaluate

Texts produced on paper usually offer familiar, socially accepted clues to their reliability and authority. Just by picking up and holding a text we can usually identify it as a book, or a letter, or a note. What signposts are there to help in our critical reading of electronic texts? How can we develop skills to evaluate, compare and criticise electronic texts as readily as we can those written on paper? New media change and develop at a bewildering rate. How can the teacher keep up to date – neither resisting change or becoming over-enthusiastic – without losing what is valuable about the culture of the past?

The ability to re-present information in different ways for different audiences

A literate adult is usually someone who can write as well as read. New media literacy, however, is often represented as purely a matter of 'reading'. Texts are broadcast, presented or delivered, and the user – child or adult – is usually seen in the single role of reader or consumer. How can we teach children to handle electronic texts as authors – web designers, multimedia creators, and so on?

The ability to use new media as a creative space

Schools are full of creative work on paper which children have originated – stories, poetry, and information texts written by children are commonplace in classroom displays. In the worlds of graphic design, music and film, the computer is commonly a creative 'workshop' – a space which encourages and enables creativity. What are the creative opportunities provided by new electronic literacies for children? How can we harness these in the process of literacy teaching?

Personalised learning

A popular ideal of many educators is what the government currently describes as 'personalised learning' in which the education system is designed to help every child to reach their full potential. There is nothing very new in this – it is what schools have always aimed to achieve. But the current ideas of personalised learning depend on ICT as a key ingredient. ICT allows a high degree of differentiated learning to take place – support for children with special needs, extension for the gifted and talented, and a whole range of day by day tools for all children to learn and create. Remote teaching by video-conferencing or electronic packages can allow easier access to shortage subjects and a wider range of skills. To quote from the 'personalised learning' document, the first principle includes e-literacy as a fundamental skill:

> for children and young people, (personalised learning) means clear learning pathways through the education system and the motivation to become independent, e-literate, fulfilled, lifelong learners.
>
> (DFES 2005, 'A national conversation about personalised learning')

Studies and research

1 Digital Rhetorics

In Australia, a large-scale two-year project entitled 'Digital Rhetorics' looked at the implications of this new world of communication technologies on the practice of literacy education. The authors have developed a useful view of what this 'new literacy' might entail. In their view, being literate has to be much more than being able to decode or encode texts; it requires a new awareness of context and the ability to create, shape and transform meanings. Education, in this view, does not just address the 'operational' literacy of making sense of print, but also needs 'cultural' and 'critical' dimensions. A child may be able to work the computer, control the tools of the word processor, and make a fair job of drafting out a piece of work, but all this may be limited to the 'operational' dimension. The 'cultural' dimension will involve the style, audience and purposes of the work, and often forms part of what we teach in school. A mature literacy, however, is able to operate in the 'critical' dimension. In the world of the internet this is the most important part:

> the ability not only to use such resources and to participate effectively and creatively in their associated cultures, but also to critique them, to read and use them against the grain, to appropriate and even re-design them.
>
> (Snyder 2003: 270)

The Digital Rhetorics study found that most educational uses of new technology – unlike the approach to paper texts – still focused almost entirely on the *operational* level of literacy.

2 Multimodal literacy

The process of learning and teaching has always used many modes of communication – writing, reading, speech, body language – and participants in learning have always developed 'literacies' to understand and create communication in these different modes. Teachers, for example, learn the body language of their pupils – and vice versa. The arrival of new technologies has added a host of new modes of discourse to the classroom, and each of these has its own 'literacy' – conventions, practices, operations and ethos. Teachers often find themselves at a disadvantage when pupils seem to be more 'literate' in these modes than they are. One of the main tasks of the literacy teacher at this time is to master these new literacies, and use them effectively in teaching and learning, so that the children they teach may be empowered and enriched by the possibilities of a multimodal learning environment.

According to Jewitt and Kress (2003) in their book *Multimodal Literacy* there has also been a perceptible shift from the traditional logic of the page to the much more visual logic of the screen. Writing has become subordinated to image. This has huge implications for teaching – from textbook design to the children's extended writing. How can we, in this cultural context, encourage children to get beyond the soundbite and factoid, and learn to create logical, connected and coherent text? And, perhaps an even greater challenge, how can we enable children to create and write within the many modes available to them – creating multimedia, websites and so on?

3 New literacies

New technologies can be used to do traditional things in a different, possibly more motivating, way. This can have a useful place in the classroom. A marker board may be better than a chalk board, and an interactive whiteboard may be an even more exciting way of doing the same thing. There is now quite a lot of research into how much of this is actually *new literacies* – or merely instances of 'old wine in new bottles'. Lankshear and Knobel (2003) observe that there is a 'deep grammar' of schooling which is very difficult to change. As soon as a new literacy enters the school environment, it rapidly becomes part of an old literacy, losing its distinctiveness and relevance to the world outside. This may happen because the school culture is teacher-directed – implying that innovation only comes from the teacher – and 'curricular' – everything taught is 'founded on texts as information sources'. So in this rather pessimistic view, school is not a good place for teaching or even engaging with new literacies. An awareness of these problems is essential if the attempt is to be made, and this book works with the assumption that it is possible to make effective and meaningful use of new technologies in the teaching of different modes of literacy.

4 Attention

Another concept which is extremely relevant to the teacher of literacy is that of attention. There is certainly no shortage of information – we are almost disappearing under the weight of it – what we are short of is 'attention' (Lankshear and Knobel 2003: 109). It is commonplace to talk about the 'short attention spans' of children. According to these authors:

> people's efforts to attract, sustain, and build attention under new media conditions … have spawned a range of new social practices and new forms of literacy associated with them.

Somebody publishes a website, advertises it. It receives a lot of visitors, and appears at the top of search lists on Google. The author has captured the attention of an audience, but also created a 'structure of attention'. But attention is not merely a matter of drawing a crowd. Information which is not attended to is just 'data' – meaningless volumes of words and numbers. The more *attention* it is given, the more meaningful and useful the information becomes. The role of the teacher of literacy, in this model, is one of encouraging attention, of increasing attention. These authors quote Lanham's powerful idea:

> that we use different terms for information depending on how much attention … has been given to it. No attention leaves us with 'raw data'. Some attention yields 'massaged data'. Lots of attention gives us 'useful information'. Maximal attention yields 'wisdom'. To simplify his argument [there is] data, information and wisdom. According to Lanham, information and wisdom are in shortest supply.

So it is important for the teacher of literacy to give priority to activities which increase attention, which develop complexity and nuance. The exercise of creativity – designing a web page or writing a poem – can be seen as making a 'structure of attention' which adds value and meaning to 'raw data'. As we have observed above, much of the use of new technology in literacy teaching is mechanical and operational – we need to find ways to use it which are much more human, multi-layered and truly literate.

5 Relationships

Children often prefer texting to talking – UK teenagers probably sent 22 billion text messages in 2005 alone (Wireless World Forum mobileYouth 2005 report, quoted in *The Guardian*, 09.06.05). According to the mobileYouth report, teenagers are 'particularly dependent on their mobile phone as a tool for social interaction' and boys who text the most in the 12–13 category outnumber girls by 3:1. This graphically illustrates the point that new technologies are primarily about communication and relationships. Lankshear and Knobel (op cit.: 106) offer a trenchant criticism of the *National Grid for Learning* initiative in the UK. To them it regards the internet as essentially a way to deliver information, whereas within the culture, the literacy, of new technologies, the internet is primarily about *relationship*. They issue the challenge:

> Schools should consider how new ICTs might be used productively in terms of relationships that could be developed and mediated using new technologies, rather than in terms of information delivery or of doing old things in new ways. (p.106)

6 Impact2

Impact2 is a major research study into the effect of ICT in schools. A vast amount of information was collected about levels of equipment in the classroom, attainment scores, and children's computer use at home and school. It demonstrated measurable positive effects of ICT on children's learning in schools which were well equipped with ICT and in which teachers engaged in good practice. A particularly interesting part of this study is the use of concept maps to get a clearer understanding of children's knowledge about ICT. It was obvious that children have a much more complex visual understanding of new media than might be expected – and this too has implications for the teaching of literacy. The Impact2 reports can be read in summary or in their entirety, along with case studies and recommendations, on the Becta site.

Further activities

For more information about the increasing research into the use of ICT, take a look at the Becta series 'What the research says about...' available in print or as downloads from the ICT Advice site. Each of these is an accessible folded A3 sheet which summarises the research evidence in a particular area of school ICT. The list is growing all the time, but currently includes the following titles which are particularly relevant to the teaching of literacy:

Leaflet 3: Portable ICT devices in teaching and learning

Leaflet 4: Virtual learning environments in teaching and learning

Leaflet 5: ICT and motivation

Leaflet 7: Interactive whiteboard

Leaflet 8: Video conferencing in teaching and learning

Leaflet 12: Supporting special educational needs (SEN) and inclusion

Leaflet 15: Digital video in teaching and learning

Leaflet 16: Using ICT in English

Leaflet 20: Classroom organisation

How to use this book

In subsequent chapters we will explore the foundation stage, whole class teaching and then guided and independent work. A chapter on ICT in different environments will give very practical help on the management of ICT and literacy in a variety of settings. Using the internet and electronic mail is addressed to the specific skills required by these new literacies – use of the world wide web and email by teacher and child. A chapter on planning and assessment will give specific resources to embed ICT in literacy teaching, and the final chapter will explore creative uses of ICT in literacy.

Each chapter starts with an overview. Where there is an overlap of content, chapters are cross-referenced. There are short case studies throughout on each subject taken from actual classroom experience. Extensive lists of web links and further reading support each section.

Web links

www.teachernet.gov.uk/wholeschool/ictis – implications of personalised learning and literacy

www.standards.dfes.gov.uk/personalisedlearning – the DfES personalised learning website

www.w2forum.com – the wireless world forum

www.guardian.co.uk – *The Guardian* newspaper

www.ngfl.gov.uk – the national grid for learning

www.becta.org.uk/research – the Impact2 research project

References

DfES (2005) 'A national conversation about personalised learning' (available from www.standards.dfes.gov.uk/personalisedlearning).

Jewitt, C. and Kress, G. (eds) (2003) *Multimodal Literacy*. New York: Peter Lang.

Lankshear, C. and Knobel, M. (2003) *New Literacies: Changing Knowledge and Classroom Learning*. Maidenhead: Open University Press.

Snyder, I. (2003) 'A new communication order: researching literacy practices in the network society', in *Language, Literacy and Education: A Reader*, S Goodman, T Lillis, J Maybin and N Mercer (eds) Stoke-on-Trent: Trentham/The Open University.

Woolgar, S. (2002) *Virtual Society? Technology, Cyberbole, Reality.* Oxford: Oxford University Press.

2

ICT in the foundation stage

Chapter overview

This chapter will look at the use of ICT in the foundation stage starting with the principles spelt out by the government foundation stage document, and how these relate to ICT. These are linked with the seven principles for good practice in early years ICT identified by early education (British Association for Early Childhood Education) in their booklet *More than Computers*. This is followed by a detailed look at the area of communication, language and literacy and some case studies of software for the early years.

Principles

The foundation stage is a time of intense activity and rapid growth in which children are constantly exploring new experiences. Alongside direct experience of the world, ICT has a powerful part to play. At the beginning of the published foundation stage guidance, the government provides a series of principles which should characterise good practice and inform teaching and learning in early years settings. Several of these – displayed in each section below – have particular implications for the use of ICT.

Provision

Children are entitled to provision that supports and extends knowledge, skills, understanding and confidence, and helps them to overcome any disadvantage.

(QCA 2000: 11)

It is very important to surround children with a rich environment in which their play can develop. In the *Guidelines for Inspection of ICT in Foundation Stage Settings*, OFSTED asks some quite rigorous questions of an early years setting:

Is adequate and varied hardware available, such as computers, printers, TV, video recorders, cassette recorders, microphones, remote control cars, and programmable floor robot? Is adequate and appropriate software available such as paint applications, a talking word processor with word bank facilities, a simple graphing package, music cassette tapes, Talking Story CD-ROMs, Adventure Games, Literacy and Numeracy activities?

The scenario implied here is filled with a wide range of ICT possibilities and choices. A 'rich' ICT setting provides a whole range of child-centred activities and pieces of equipment which children can use in many different ways to extend and develop their experience. This is an important part of the richness and diversity of early childhood education.

Some practitioners have expressed a certain reluctance to engage with too much ICT, because of their distrust of computers. Their understanding is that electronic or virtual experience is always a poor second to direct experience of the world. While priority should always be given to actual touching, handling, using the senses, engaging with the real world, it is also true that the 'real world' includes many forms of ICT. Many activities can become richer as children begin to use electronic media for imaginative play and symbol making, and many forms of ICT enable children to create and manipulate things which would otherwise be impossible. ICT activities should in no way replace more traditional experiences of the world, but can have value in extending these experiences.

Learning often comes about as a direct result of children's intuitive interaction with the setting's environment. There is an occasion for learning whenever the child's natural motivation to explore and find out meets the rich environment planned and set up by the practitioner. The early years setting should include a wealth of objects and activities connected with ICT, and these will provide many occasions for learning particularly in the area of communication.

SureStart's list of ICT includes not just computers, but activity centres, musical keyboards, play telephones and tape recorders, radio-controlled toys, talking toys, video tapes, telephones, fax machines, television, walkie talkies, kitchen appliances, dictating machines, and even metal detectors! This list is by no means exhaustive. All of these devices provide powerful opportunities for communication and role play. The computer itself can also offer a huge variety of software and child-appropriate websites which are catalysts for learning.

Building on experience

Early years experience should build on what children already know and can do. It should also encourage a positive attitude and disposition to learn and aim to prevent early failure.
(QCA 2000: 11)

Many children whose homes are rich in ICT come into the setting with a great deal of prior experience of ICT devices of all kinds. They will already be able to go far beyond the fairly cautious statements of the early learning goals and will probably do things with a computer which appear quite adult and sophisticated. Other children may have no experience at all – the keyboard may be a daunting and frightening object, and they may avoid ICT in favour of more reassuring and cuddly playthings. The practitioner needs to be able to support both of these cases.

An effort should be made to establish some continuity between home and school, and any home experiences the children have will naturally support what they do in school. While it is important for the practitioner to build on this prior experience, it is even more vital to be proactive in compensating those children who are from the other side of the 'digital divide' and who may have no prior experience of ICT at all. Equal opportunity in this case will require positive intervention on behalf of these children, and this needs to be made explicit in planning – it is very easy for children to be overlooked.

Inclusion

> Practitioners should ensure that all children feel included, secure and valued…No child should be excluded or disadvantaged because of ethnicity, culture or religion, home language, family background, special educational needs, disability, gender or ability.
>
> (QCA 2000: 11)

For children with special needs, ICT can be a positive and affirming force for inclusion – providing resources and ways of access to learning materials. This is most obvious where ICT makes an immediate and practical contribution to communication in speech or writing. A child with very weak muscular control may use a switch to operate the screen pointer of a computer to type or sound out words. Children who lack the precise coordination required to operate a keyboard or mouse may use alternatives such as speech input, a touch screen which responds to hand contact, or a sound-beam which controls a computer by gesture. Access technology such as this highlights a constant theme in the use of ICT at any level: ICT enables and empowers the user to do things which would otherwise be difficult or impossible. This sense of empowerment, granting independence and autonomy to children, is an essential contribution that ICT makes to the curriculum. In summary, ICT enables me to do things I cannot do without it. Here are some simple examples of this which apply to children in the early years – but also to adults!

ICT enables me to…

- Converse with people out of earshot (telephone)
- See things which are distant in space or time (television)
- Hear a story I have told, a song I have sung (tape recorder)
- Find information from anywhere in the world (the internet)
- Form a letter perfectly by pressing a key (word processor)
- Try out a design in lots of different colours (paint programs)

Play

> There should be opportunities for children to engage in activities planned by adults and also those that they plan or initiate themselves. Children do not make a distinction between 'play' and 'work' and neither should practitioners. Children need time to become engrossed, work in depth and complete activities.
>
> (QCA 2000: 11)

ICT resources still exert a certain fascination on children. They evoke a high degree of attention and concentration, and can therefore provide occasions for children to play in ways which are highly motivating and extending. An ICT device, such as a digital camera, can in itself be an engrossing and motivating catalyst for learning. With teacher intervention, it can become part of all kinds of role play. Bear in mind that some of the most useful devices in ICT-related play can be such things as toy mobile phones. These enable the child to play out the implications of ICT in role as a user, developing appropriate language, and acting out the conventions of handling and control of the device.

An actual computer – working or not – can be a very useful catalyst for play. Obviously, children need to be aware of the fragile nature of electrical devices, but this in itself can be a meaningful part of play, where careful handling is modelled by the practitioner. The computer can 'act' the part of a real-life computer in a world where every shop or office has a computer on the desk. If the computer works, and a program is set up where the child can 'type', this may well be enough.

There are also children's programs designed for role play, where the computer has the kind of material on the screen that might be seen in a real life setting. The Semerc series of role play CDs (At the Vet's, Café, Doctor's, Garden Centre, Toy Shop and Post Office) is an excellent example of these (available from www.onestopeducation.co.uk). These programs are simple and effective. At the Vet's and At the Doctor's medicine is taken out of the cupboard, and various pieces of equipment such as stethoscopes, and X-rays are used to diagnose and treat the patient. Brief animations and sounds encourage the child to click on items and see what happens, while remaining in role as a vet, animal or worried patient.

Next steps

> Practitioners must be able to observe and respond appropriately to children, informed by a knowledge of how children develop and learn and a clear understanding of possible next steps in their development and learning.
>
> (QCA 2000: 11)

A good practitioner is always on the lookout for the 'next step' which will add to and develop a child's learning. Sometimes this will be a new activity, sometimes an extended or elaborated version of what is taking place, and sometimes the same activity in a different form. If she makes the 'next step' an ICT activity, this can also become a way to encourage meaningful encounters with different modalities of learning.

As an example, handling and sorting of real objects on the carpet can be followed by a 'virtual' activity which involves dragging pictures using the mouse. Although the child is apparently doing the same sort of thing, the activity which now appears in a virtual form on the computer screen uses a whole different range of symbols, meanings and skills. Symbols are interpreted and links are being made. Pictures are *representing* objects. A movement of the hand on the mouse mat is *representing* a movement on the screen, and so on. This is one way in which ICT activities do not have to replace direct experience, but can enrich it into different expressions.

Intervention

> Well-planned, purposeful activity and appropriate intervention by practitioners will engage children in the learning process and help them make progress in their learning.
>
> (QCA 2000: 11)

An intervention which extends the moment of learning by introducing an ICT extension activity can be very powerful and effective. This obviously requires a practitioner to be aware of all the different ICT possibilities available. It may also take full advantage of the intrinsic motivation which is provided by ICT resources, which can engross children and take their learning to a higher level.

It is often noticed that even in those settings which are rich in ICT resources, only a few children engage with them fully, and some children may miss out on ICT activities altogether. This may be caused by children coming into the setting with very different levels of confidence or prior experience at home. As with any other successful early years teaching, intervention is critical. ICT activities will only be of any value if the practitioner notices, values, encourages and develops their use. This is essentially an issue of inclusion – all children deserve the rich experiences which can be offered through the effective use of ICT.

Planning

> For children to have rich and stimulating experiences, the learning environment should be well planned and well organised. It provides the structure for teaching within which children explore, experiment, plan and make decisions for themselves, thus enabling them to learn, develop and make good progress.
>
> (QCA 2000: 12)

The ICT objects, activities and programs provided for the children need to be planned with sensitivity and understanding. A single program 'left on' – always available on a computer screen – does not provide for choice or appropriate 'match' to the learning needs of different children. All levels of planning documentation should include ICT as a matter of course. This will include equipment to be available at each appropriate session – computer, camera, tape recorder, programmable toys and so on – but also some activities which encourage the children to use these. 'ICT' equipment will include objects which do not work, but which have an important part to play as role-play props – old telephones, cardboard televisions, discarded computer keyboards and mice.

Good planning will also offer leading questions and suggestions for practitioners to extend any theme into an ICT direction as part of the natural flow of learning in the setting.

Knowledgeable practitioners

> Above all, effective learning and development for young children requires high-quality care and education by practitioners. Effective education requires both a relevant curriculum and practitioners who understand and are able to implement the curriculum requirements.

> (QCA 2000: 12)

Effective use of ICT in foundation settings requires a particular type of knowledge in the practitioner, which can appear very daunting to an outsider. All the adults who participate in sessions need to be sufficiently confident in ICT to help the children appropriately. However, this does not imply a high degree of knowledge about computers: it is 'local' and specific knowledge which is the most important. The teaching assistant or parent must be encouraged to find out about the ICT in the setting, but also to have an attitude of play and experiment which will grow alongside the children. She does not need to know everything about all types of ICT, but she does need knowledge and confidence of every available resource which is available in the immediate environment of the setting. Without this knowledge, the ICT experiences offered may rapidly become repetitive and without challenge. The most vital knowledge is that which enables the practitioner to guide a child into the most appropriate ICT activity to extend their learning – the best next step.

Observation

As children make their first steps into literacy, the practitioner's observation and recording is crucial. The most exciting growth happens in moments of role play, or in passing conversations which are very easily missed and overlooked. The recording aspects of ICT can have a huge part to play in capturing process. A digital camera, video camera, sound recorder – all these can freeze moments of process and allow the practitioner to evaluate, assess and celebrate the moment or share it with the parent.

Seven principles

More than Computers, an invaluable booklet from Early Education (British Association for Early Childhood Education) identifies seven general principles for the effective use of ICT in early years settings. I will relate these briefly to the communication/literacy areas of experience. They are:

1 Ensure an educational purpose

Some parents, and even some teachers, are happy to see a computer switched on – with some children sitting in front of it. They make the assumption that something educational is happening, that learning is occurring, but this may not be the case. 'Educational' software may be pitched at too high a level of language or may present no challenge at all. Many 'drill and practice' programs actually do nothing but test children. If the child picks – by knowledge or trial and error – the correct word or picture, the computer gives them noisy feedback. This is almost always a waste of time in terms of learning. If children are able to answer the question, they probably don't need to – they would be better doing something else. If they cannot answer the question, they will not learn from a computer screen. They will probably click on items at random until something happens – a way of passing the time, admittedly, but of no educational value.

Check questions

Always approach the encounter between child and computer with a critical attitude. Ask questions such as these:

- Is the interest level appropriate for this child?
- Is the content level appropriate for this child?
- Do these two levels match each other?
- What are the children actually *doing* when they use this?
- Would they be better employed in a 'real-life' version of this activity?
- What do I hope to achieve with the children who are using this software?
- Are there opportunities for creativity, self-expression and language-extending talk?

Role play is often the most educational use of ICT – either with real, working pieces of equipment, or with toys for pretend play.

2 Encourage collaboration

Language is developed above all in communication. Almost any activity at a computer screen becomes more effective if an adult is involved – intervening now and then with open questions, extending vocabulary, encouraging conversation. As mentioned above, the 'virtuality' of computer software leads to conversations which naturally include symbol-making.

In a study by Helen Finlayson and Deirdre Cook (1998) groups of children used a 'My world' activity with blocks – on screen and in the 'real world.' The authors were exploring the value of what they called 'passive software' – where the children structure the activity themselves. They found:

When working on the computer:

- The sessions lasted longer.

- The children were more involved in their partner's work.

- They were less open to general distractions.

- They developed the tasks further or showed greater persistence.

- They showed greater enthusiasm for the task.

All of these factors mean that collaborative work around a computer or piece of ICT equipment can really help to support language development.

If the setting has an interactive whiteboard, placed at such a height that the children can access it easily, the scope for collaboration increases. A group of children can control the computer with space to move and interact. The movements in 'dressing a teddy' or moving pictures about involve the whole body and are much more satisfying than tiny mouse movements. Any activity you carry out on a computer screen can be performed as easily on the interactive whiteboard. For a fuller account of interactive whiteboards and their use in the classroom see Chapter 5.

Check questions

- Do the ICT activities in my setting encourage collaboration?

- How can I enrich the quality of interaction and conversation around these activities?

- Are there any ways in which I can make ICT equipment more accessible?

3 Integrate with other aspects of curriculum

ICT is not to be used in isolation – use the ICT in the setting to add value to the other communication activities taking place. If there is a shop set up for role play, could the computer, with an appropriate piece of software, be playing a part in that scenario? Programs such as 'At the vet's' (Semerc) are perfect for this. ICT devices, including the computer, are best seen as tools which are used when they add value to an activity – not in a rota, not as a reward.

Check questions

- Do I routinely set up ICT activities in the role play areas?
- Are digital cameras and control toys always available, or just on 'special' occasions?

4 Ensure that the child is in control

The concept of 'active software' and 'passive software' mentioned above is very important. 'Arcade games' are a classic example of 'active software' – the child responds, as rapidly as possible, to what is presented on the screen, and is tested by the program. A 'paint' program, by contrast, is passive – it only does what the child initiates. In general, in an early years setting, the child should wherever possible be able to take control of the software, learning to be autonomous, to make choices and develop understanding. The language development of an active, autonomous learner is far richer than that of a passive learner.

Check questions

- How 'active' are the children – mentally and physically – in their engagement with ICT in my setting?
- Is there any software I should introduce to give children control?
- Is there any software I should sideline because it keeps the children 'passive' in their learning?

5 Choose applications that are transparent

Steve Jobs, founder of Apple Computers, once worked as a designer for Atari Games machines. The manual was simple: 'turn on, play'. Not all software is as easy as that! It is vital that the ICT hardware and software we offer to young children has this quality of 'transparency' – that the screens are intuitive and logical, that they work in the way children's minds work.

There is a perennial problem with the early stages of word-processing. A keyboard is an incredibly complex structure of letters – in an order which is completely mysterious. The letters are also usually presented in upper case, whereas children start to read words in lower case. There are several ways in which early writing on the computer can be made more transparent:

- Use 'lower-case' keyboards (or overlays or stickers)

- Avoid or reduce the use of a keyboard by using a program such as Clicker which provides word banks. In Clicker, a 'grid' on the screen contains letters or words. Clicking these 'drops' them into a word-processor without the need to use a keyboard at all.

- Computers are increasingly able to understand speech and handwriting, and it is very likely that the children we teach may come to view keyboards as a thing of the past.

Check questions

- Can I make children's access to ICT more simple and intuitive?
- Look carefully at the software you use in your setting. Discuss it with the children:
  - What is hard to do?
  - What is really easy?
  - What would you like it to be able to do if you had three wishes?

6 Avoid applications containing violence or stereotyping

Always be sensitive to the content of games and programs – they may not be promoting the values you would wish to promote. A computer game whose content is designed to teach letter sounds or simple numbers may have a scenario which involves shooting down aliens. What 'story' does the child take away from the program? What are they actually learning here? It is possible that some programs may emphasise scores and competition more explicitly than learning. The pictures of children on-screen may be different in culture or ethnic group from the children who are using the program. Many early years settings run on a very tight budget, and may welcome CD-Roms or software packages which are donated to them without first checking their suitability. There are no hard and fast rules in all this, but it is important to maintain a critical attitude to the values embedded in software for children.

7 Be aware of health and safety issues

In society at large, there are serious concerns about the effect of spending hours in front of computer screens, particularly in offices. Repetitive use of keyboards, particularly when these are badly positioned, can lead to muscle strain (repetitive strain injury – RSI). TV and computer screens also carry a small risk of radiation, and children should be discouraged from spending time too close to them. Furniture should allow children to adopt a good upright posture when typing or using a mouse. Fortunately, these risks will have very little effect in early years settings as children usually have such a brief exposure to computers. When using interactive whiteboards, children need to be warned not to look into the beam, as it may cause eye damage. This is quite easy to avoid. Children will generally avoid the discomfort by playing safe – as they learn quickly not to look directly at the sun.

Always be aware that some children find it hard to see fine detail on a screen. Use high contrast text wherever possible, and ensure that icons and symbols are as large as possible. White on black is often clearer in projection than black on white. Children with visual problems may not cope with multicoloured screens or those filled with animated text and figures.

Check questions

- Is equipment safely set up, with no trailing wires or unprotected sockets?
- Are children aware of the danger of dazzle from projector beams?
- Are children encouraged to sit well at the computer?
- Are ICT issues included on our health and safety policy?

Unpacking the area of communication, language and literacy

Communication

This section is based on the QCA/DfEE *Curriculum guidance for the foundation stage* (2000) relevant extracts of which appear in italics.

> *Interaction with others, negotiating plans and activities and taking turns in conversation.*
> (QCA 2000: 48)

Simple 'games' activities provide a focus for conversation and interaction, and encourage turn-taking. This is also true of ICT equipment such as digital cameras. A typical activity might involve showing a group of children a digital camera, allowing them to explore and control it for themselves, then taking a series of pictures of the setting. At its best, this activity will encourage all kinds of purposeful exchanges and negotiations. To use such a device is highly motivating, and will encourage turn-taking, as well as creating a 'product' which in turn will stimulate a lot of rich and meaningful talk.

Case study

On a visit to a working farm, a group of three children were allowed to use the digital camera. They had each used the camera before, and knew how to turn it on, use the viewfinder and press the button to take a picture. One child had the responsibility for carrying the camera and ensuring that the loop of the handle stayed round her wrist. They negotiated who would have the first 'go' and were able to take turns without too much conflict. They were asked to take some pictures of all the different kinds of animals that they would see during their visit. Using the camera stimulated their conversation about the animals, and they took a great deal of care getting each picture the way they wanted it to be. The adult with the group encouraged them to take several pictures of each animal.

In all this they were developing a concept and understanding that the pictures were stored 'inside' the camera, that they could 'play them back' on the camera, but that they could also be moved onto the computer screen to show everybody else. When they returned to school the whole group watched a slide-show of the visit, giving rise to further and richer talk, and deepening their experience by creating a fuller narrative together.

- Significant moments from the visit were captured by using ICT, and could be named and discussed.
- Children learnt operational skills and technical language (button, switch, viewfinder, click, and so on).
- The camera gave rise to negotiating and turn-taking conversations.
- The sequence of pictures – in taking and viewing – strengthened the children's sense of time and order of events.
- Children learnt – at a simple level – about data transfer between ICT devices.

Possible extension activities

- The teacher or an older child inserts the pictures into a word processor or DTP program and makes posters to display.
- Working with an adult, a group use Photo Story to make a presentation, and record a commentary together. They show it to other classes.

Language for communication

Talking books

Sustain attentive listening, responding to what they have heard by relevant comments, questions or actions.

(QCA 2000: 50)

Listen with enjoyment, and respond to stories, songs and other music, rhymes and poems and make up their own stories, songs, rhymes and poems.

(QCA 2000: 50)

Extend their vocabulary, exploring the meanings and sounds of new words.

(QCA 2000: 50)

ICT offers many texts which combine speech and words, and these can reinforce the link between written and spoken text. There are many talking stories available – on CD and the internet. Usually they combine a presentation of text and pictures, often animated, with a computer reading of the text. This reading can be either of the whole text, or individual words which can be clicked to read. Some stories have 'sampled' voices – in effect recordings of real actors reading the text. Others have 'software speech' a synthesised robot-like voice produced by the computer itself. The practitioner must decide whether the speech in a particular story actually models speech they want the children to use. These talking books are obviously designed to encourage early reading, but should be approached with a certain amount of caution.

Reading and listening to a story is an engagement with a text, but it is set firmly within a framework of communication between people. When a mother sits her child on her knee and they read a story, it is not primarily about decoding together – the context is one of intimacy and shared experience. A computer 'talking book' preserves some elements of this experience, but others are entirely lost. It is possible that the animations, sound effects, 'bells and whistles' of electronic story books are an attempt to engage the child and hold their attention in the absence of intimacy and interpersonal communication.

From the point of view of the foundation stage setting, the implication is that a talking story is most useful if it can be shared between an adult and a child, or group of children. It is doubtful whether the talking story by itself can be as effective as a shared electronic text.

Some talking books

Here is a brief selection from the many CD-Rom 'talking books' available which are suitable for younger children. They are very variable in content and quality, and many publishers seem to have abandoned the format as the initial production costs are very high. The following titles may be purchased from Amazon or REM, but this is only an indicative list:

- Dr Seuss, *Cat in the Hat* (Dorling Kindersley – now GSP)
- Dr Seuss, *Green Eggs and Ham* (Softkey)
- *Just Grandma and Me* (Broderbund)
- *Little Polar Bear Interactive Storybook* (Dorling Kindersley)

- *Oxford Reading Tree* (Oxford University Press)
- *Rainbow Fish and The Whale Interactive Storybook* (Dorling Kindersley)
- *Story Studio Winnie The Pooh and Tigger Too* (Disney Interactive)
- *The Jolly Post Office* (Dorling Kindersley – now GSP)
- *The Snowman Interactive Storybook* (FastTrak)

Internet activity

Curriculum Online has already developed into a valuable gateway to many resources for teaching communication, language and literacy in the foundation stage. It can be searched by age group and subject area, and provides links to free products or to suppliers and reviewers of products which are commercially available. All the resources on Curriculum Online have to meet certain criteria of quality, and they can be purchased using electronic learning credits (eLCs). Find Curriculum online at http://www.curriculumonline.gov.uk

Language for thinking

Use language to imagine and recreate roles and experiences.

(QCA 2000: 58)

Use talk to organise, sequence and clarify thinking, ideas, feelings and events.

(QCA 2000: 58)

The computer can provide a powerful focus within role-play activities. In real life, there is a computer on every desk – for the travel agent's database, the dentist's booking system, or the vet's medication records. Using the computer for these roles in play – with or without specific software – can engage the child in activities in which information is collected or received.

Other ICT devices, real or pretend, can have a major role in imaginative play. The excellent Early Education publication, *More than Computers* points out that a 'pretend mobile telephone' can be a much more effective catalyst of learning than many expensive pieces of computer software whose educational value is limited or non-existent.

Linking sounds and letters

Hear and say initial and final sounds in words, and short vowel sounds within words.

(QCA 2000: 60)

Link sounds to letters, naming and sounding the letters of the alphabet.

(QCA 2000: 60)

Use their phonic knowledge to write simple regular words and make phonetically plausible attempts at more complex words.

(QCA 2000: 60)

There are many software packages which offer 'drill and practice' activities to reinforce a child's beginning knowledge of phonics. Some are well designed and motivating to children, and children usually enjoy using them. They have severe limitations, however, only reinforcing what a child already knows. You will find more detail on planning early language activities in Chapter 7.

Language for reading

Explore and experiment with sounds, words and texts.

(QCA 2000: 62)

Retell narratives in the correct sequence, drawing on language patterns of stories.

(QCA 2000: 62)

Read a range of familiar and common words and simple sentences independently.

(QCA 2000: 62)

Know that print carries meaning and, in English, is read from left to right and top to bottom.

(QCA 2000: 62)

Show an understanding of the elements of stories, such as main character, sequence of events, and openings, and how information can be found in non-fiction texts to answer questions about where, who, why and how.

(QCA 2000: 62)

The interactive whiteboard allows an unprecedented sharing of texts, many of which are available online. As the technology is still quite new, many teachers use what is easily available. Unfortunately the quality of many online and CD-Rom texts is far inferior to the stories and books available in print. It is vital to evaluate all texts from the point of view of their quality and appropriateness for the children's learning, rather than their electronic presentation. A good book is always better than a bad CD-Rom!

Language for writing

Use their phonic knowledge to write simple regular words and make phonetically plausible attempts at more complex words.

(QCA 2000: 60 and 64)

Attempt writing for different purposes, using features of different forms such as lists, stories and instructions.

(QCA 2000: 64)

Write their own names and other things such as labels and captions and begin to form simple sentences, sometimes using punctuation.

(QCA 2000: 64)

Children enjoy 'typing' on a computer keyboard long before they can write, and this too is an important part of play. When they begin to write or copy meaningful words a talking word-processor or word-bank program such as Clicker is invaluable. It provides instant and motivating feedback, and enables a child to *communicate* using writing at a higher level than they would otherwise be able to achieve.

Software for early years

There is an unwritten philosophy in some parts of the education system that a suite of 'Office' programs – as found in many home, commercial and business settings – is an adequate software resource for children. Typically this will include a word-processor, a desk-top publishing program, a spreadsheet and possibly a database – all at adult level. Unfortunately this even happens in some early years settings, particularly where computers have been donated or passed on from commercial settings. Commercial business software is designed to increase productivity, and new versions come out every year with features that are added primarily because a software designer is able to create them – most of which are never used by most people. Practitioners can make valiant efforts to render the software suitable for the activities they have in mind – enlarging and removing icons, installing 'child-friendly' fonts and so on – but this is work that should really be avoided by purchasing more appropriate software.

At the opposite extreme, there is a growing range of software which has been designed starting from the needs of children, usually in consultation with teachers. In the UK scene two prime examples of this have been Clicker (from Crick software) and the various packages from 2Simple. This section will look more closely at some of this software and the thinking behind it, exploring some of the implications for those who design software and those who select it for use in children's learning. This is not to suggest that these are the only pieces of software appropriate to use, but to underline the design and access principles which should inform the choice of software.

Case study: toolkits for early years ICT

Many practitioners find it convenient to buy one 'toolkit' software package which will supply them with the main applications they need for one age group. There are now many products like this. This section will look more closely at a fairly typical early years suite of programs, 'Numbers, Words and Pictures 2'. This includes a very simple database and graph-making program, a turtle logo package, a sorting program, an easy 'painting' program and one literacy item – Writer 2.

One advantage of a suite like this is that children can use skills learnt in one program in one of the others, as they all have the same 'look and feel.' Writer 2 offers very simple writing tasks in the form of layouts or templates – a story with a picture, a postcard and so on.

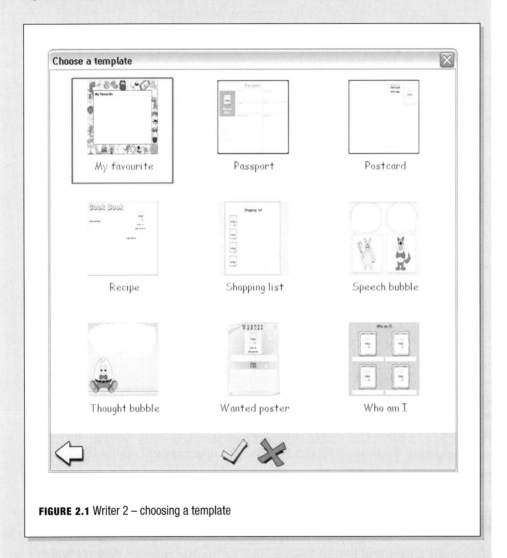

FIGURE 2.1 Writer 2 – choosing a template

Children can choose pictures from a collection. They can insert pre-set words from a word bank, and listen to their writing using computer-generated speech.

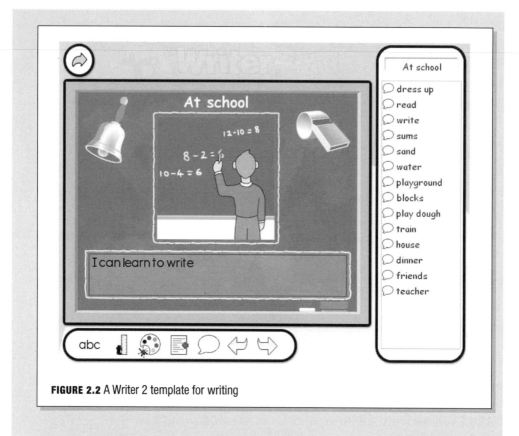

FIGURE 2.2 A Writer 2 template for writing

With software like this, it is very easy to carry out small and self-contained pieces of writing.

Case study: 2Create a Story – multimedia software for early literacy

2Create a Story takes a fresh and innovative approach to early writing, bringing the multimedia possibilities of new technology to children's story making. A child draws a picture on the screen using paint tools, and then writes a short sentence for a story beneath it. But then with very simple tools children can make the picture appear and disappear, rock from side to side, or scatter into pieces. They can choose appropriate sounds, or record their own with a microphone plugged into the computer. Having made one 'page', they can start a new one, then watch the whole story unroll as a multimedia presentation.

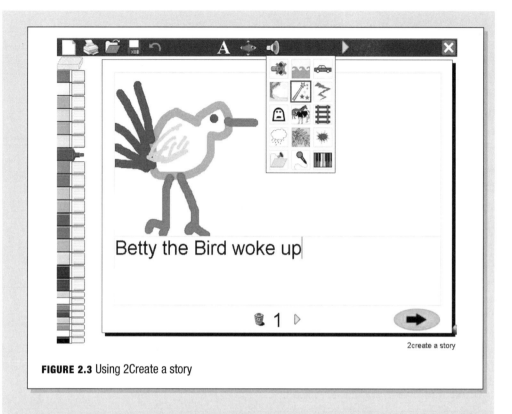

FIGURE 2.3 Using 2Create a story

Until very recently, multimedia creation like this would have been quite an advanced procedure – now it is available to children in the foundation stage. Children are able to create their stories, not with an on-screen representation of paper – but really engaging with the new literacies required by new technologies.

The program 2Create takes this further – each page behaves as a separate 'card' and can be linked in different ways to other cards to make branching stories. All the techniques needed are explained very clearly on video animations of the program which come with the package.

2Create a Story exemplifies a healthy approach to software design – starting from the perceived needs of children, and designing to meet them as simply as possible. A good deal of educational software seems to be an attempt to replicate printed media, or scale down an 'adult' program for children's use. For an adult user, a 'simple' program may seem limited – there are no choices of font size, few 'drawing' tools and so on. But this simplicity focuses children on the key educational objectives in a motivating and exciting way.

Case study: word banks and grids

Clicker has become a standard package in schools for children with special needs, and also children in the first stages of learning to write. Its success has been based on continuous feedback from teachers which has been incorporated into the design of the program. When computers first appeared in schools, concept keyboards were a very common sight. These are A4 or A3 size boards, covered with a paper overlay. Children could press a word on the paper, and it would appear on the screen, allowing them to write without using the keyboard. Clicker took this idea onto the computer screen. At the bottom of a typical word-processor page there is a 'grid' of words or pictures. Click one of these with the right-hand mouse button, and it speaks. Click it with the left and it drops into the word-processor. A 'cell' in a grid can also call up another grid, so that a few clicks can give quick access to a huge vocabulary. This has been liberating for children with special needs, particularly those who are unable to communicate verbally, as with a simple switch or pointer, they can speak and write effectively.

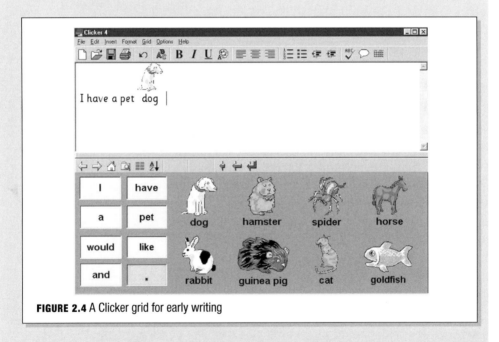

FIGURE 2.4 A Clicker grid for early writing

Since this was designed from first principles, starting from the needs of children, it rapidly became an indispensable support for early literacy. Customised grids are very easy to create, and a whole sub-culture of lesson materials has developed. Learning grids are now exchanged online and provide a vast resource of literacy materials. Clicker has developed all kinds of different functions, but still remains simple and relevant.

Future developments

The current 'Birth to three' (2005) agenda and the ongoing transformation of schools into extended schools and children's centres will have a huge impact on the culture and practice of UK schools. This is a great opportunity for software developers and teachers to develop materials which support and enable children in the areas of play, creativity and communication, while safeguarding interpersonal contact. ICT in early years has an enormous contribution to make to the growth of truly literate children.

Web links

http://www.onestopeducation.co.uk – details on the Semerc 'At the ...' series

http://www.curriculumonline.gov.uk – curriculum online

http://www.cricksoft.com/uk – information on Clicker

http://www.2simple.com – 2Simple software

References

Becta (2005) 'Guidelines for inspection of ICT in foundation stage settings'. Web reference: http://www.becta.org.uk/corporate/corporate.cfm?section=1&id=2050

Finlayson, H. and Cook, D. (1998) 'The value of passive software in young children's collaborative work' in *IT for Learning Enhancement*. Monteith, M. (ed.) (1998) Exeter: Intellect Books.

QCA/DfES (2000) *Curriculum Guidance for the Foundation Stage*. London: DfES.

Siraj-Blatchford, I. and Siraj-Blatchford, J. (2003) *More than Computers: Information and Communication Technology in the Early Years*. London: Early Education.

SureStart/DfES (2005) *Primary National Strategy. Notes for participants in one-day events: ICT in the Foundation Stage*. London: DfES.

Whitehead, M.R. (2004) *Language and Literacy in the Early Years*, 3rd edn, London: Sage.

3

Whole class teaching using ICT

Chapter overview

Whole class teaching in literacy sessions and across the curriculum is a feature of primary teaching at the beginning of the twenty-first century. Presentational tools such as the digital projector or interactive whiteboard are much more widely available, providing new uses of technology to support lessons. ICT has much to offer teachers and trainee teachers as a tool to support and enhance learning during whole class sessions. It is also a means of providing a new dimension in terms of different kinds of texts and new audiences and purposes for writing. This chapter will start by discussing the range of ways that ICT can be used in whole class teaching and will consider the range of appropriate hardware. Relevant research and inspection evidence will be discussed as well as inclusion issues in whole class teaching, and examples will be given to illustrate creative and practical ways of using ICT in literacy teaching.

A background to whole class teaching and the national literacy strategy

Whole class teaching was an essential feature of the literacy hour introduced by the National Literacy Strategy (NLS) in 1998 for children at key stage 1 and key stage 2 in England. This document provided guidance for schools and gave more detail of how to implement the statutory requirements of the National Curriculum (DfEE/QCA 1999). Prior to the introduction of the NLS, concerns had been expressed by some educational thinkers about the quality of primary teaching. A discussion paper commonly referred to as 'The Three Wise Men's Report' noted that 'there is insufficient exploitation of the benefits of whole class teaching' (DES 1992: 2) in primary schools. The NLS Framework (DfEE 1998) attempted to remedy this and gave a rationale for a clear focus on what is called 'literacy instruction' delivered through whole class and group teaching. The idea was that pupils should benefit from the maximum possible teaching time as well as acquiring independent learning skills. However, the point is made in the framework that whole class teaching is not a return to 'transmission teaching'.

More recently there has been a relaxation of the demands on schools to follow NLS guidance to the letter. However, whole class teaching is still widely used as a strategy for teaching literacy, and whole class teaching continues to be promoted by the document *Excellence and Enjoyment* (DfES 2003a) and the Primary Strategy. On the other hand, the quality of this whole class teaching can not necessarily be assured. Whole class teaching was promoted by the NLS as an active method of teaching although in practice this has not always been the case, as noted by English *et al.* (2002). These researchers found that pupils rarely contribute more extended thoughts and ideas in whole class sessions. The use of ICT does not necessarily mean that whole class teaching is any more active or participatory but it may add resources which actively engage and motivate pupils. The Primary Strategy's speaking and listening guidance (DfES 2003b) also goes some way to addressing the issues of lack of interactivity and lack of opportunities for ICT in the literacy hour.

The emphasis on whole class teaching at the time of the introduction of the NLS in many ways caused a dropping off in the frequency of ICT use. As the NLS was being introduced, funding was also provided to support training for all primary teachers in the curricular and pedagogical uses of ICT. Literacy and ICT were both given a very high profile by the government and yet, in practice, teachers found it hard to balance the demand for more whole class teaching with an emphasis on using new technologies to promote literacy learning.

The role of ICT was largely ignored in the NLS framework. There were few explicit references in the framework or training materials (MAPE 1998). Teachers needed to reassess how ICT could be used in a situation in which it was not possible to give pupils access to computers for a sustained period during the literacy hour structure. The short-term response was to neglect the use of ICT to teach literacy. However, the tools available in classrooms have changed remarkably since the introduction of the NLS and many teachers have regular access to interactive whiteboards, computers and data projectors and computer suites to support the teaching of literacy. There have been changes to the resources available but the issue of ensuring that ICT is at least considered as an appropriate tool during whole class teaching still remains one that needs to be addressed.

Using ICT in whole class teaching

This next section gives an overview of how to use ICT for whole class work. The following list summarises possible ICT use.

- A presentation or stimulus
- Presenting texts
- Demonstration

ns

ructions

eas

ideo and cine clips

A presentation or stimulus

Presentations on themes connected with literacy teaching can be made by copying and pasting illustrations and text from the internet and then editing the text to make it more suitable for the needs of particular groups. The teacher can create a stimulus at the beginning of a unit of work. For example, the theme might be stories by the same author and the teacher could create a presentation on an author which uses snippets of video, illustrations and extracts from books to be studied.

Presenting texts

Any word-processed texts can easily be displayed, discussed, text marked and manipulated using a computer linked to a projector or an interactive whiteboard. Children's own texts can be used as well as texts created with pupils during sessions or teachers' initial ideas can be changed or reworked. Brainstorming can be presented and the results saved and returned to during a later lesson. Texts can be saved, reworked and returned to through several stages of editing and publishing. Two texts can be compared and manipulated using a split screen. As well as more traditional texts, ICT texts such as web pages and CD-Roms can be discussed and created as part of whole class teaching.

Demonstration

ICT can be used to demonstrate particular teaching points – for example, how to combine different chunks or morphemes to spell a word, how to use an electronic dictionary or thesaurus, how to use a writing frame which contains connectives that knit a text together or how to set out play scripts with stage directions and speech.

Explanations

ICT can be used to support explanations – for example, the need for grammatical agreement can be demonstrated using a word-processor where ungrammatical forms are text marked; a text can be scrolled and passages that explain a particular character's behaviour can be highlighted.

Giving instructions

ICT can replace the need for handwritten lists or handouts. Instructions can easily be returned to whereas on a conventional whiteboard they will have been erased.

Literacy and ICT in th

requi
ra

Linking ideas

Concept maps can be created using ICT that links ideas, for
map to support character analysis when reading a narrative
which forms an overview of a text.

Using video and cine clips

Many video clips are available and can be used to enhance children's understanding of visual literacy and to make links with print literacy. Clips can also provide a
stimulus for writing. A short piece of film can be shown to the children to help them
to create the setting for a piece of narrative writing. Many children find this particularly difficult. A dramatic film clip which contains atmospheric lighting and
sound effects can support children to write more vividly and creatively.

Hardware considerations

It is possible to use one computer with the whole class with an enlarged monitor or
data projector, and a screen or interactive whiteboard. Computer suites also have a
place in whole class presentations as pupils can interact at their own screen as the
teacher demonstrates. A wireless mouse or tablet PC can also enable interactive
whole class teaching and demonstration. The broader definition of ICT tools also
includes items like tape recorders and audio players, televisions, videos and DVD
recorders and players, all of which can be used successfully in whole class teaching.

digital
cameras?
Roamers?

Shared work in the National Literacy Strategy

The next section takes the three components of whole class teaching contained in
the NLS framework: shared reading, shared writing and whole class word and
sentence level teaching. Each element is discussed in turn with specific examples of
practice.

Shared reading

Whole class teaching of reading in many literacy lessons takes place through the
practice of shared reading. This involves working with the whole class using a
shared text which may often be a big book, particularly at key stage 1. Using
enlarged texts was pioneered in the work of Don Holdaway (1979). Holdaway
emphasised the importance of teachers modelling reading strategies for children.
However, whatever strategies are used, a key factor in the success of shared reading
is providing a sufficiently clear view of the text so that all children can be involved.
ICT can help in providing clear images. The text may be a big book but there are
many other sources of texts, including ICT texts. The texts recommended by the
NLS cover poems, advertisements, short extracts, leaflets and newspaper articles,
and so on. Traditional chronological texts alone cannot cover the range of material

red. ICT can be used to provide access to suitable texts and to expand the range of types of texts.

Shared reading can be enriched by the use of two types of ICT texts. The first type consists of traditional books presented electronically. The second type includes ICT texts which are read in a completely different way. In the first type of text the reader moves in a left to right direction through the texts but they have additional features such as moving illustrations and text that 'talks' to the reader. Some schools now use electronic versions of big books or text extracts on interactive whiteboards. The advantage of these is that text can be easily transformed and teachers and pupils can record their interactions with a text by highlighting key words or phrases, making notes on screen or hiding key aspects of a text. Interactive whiteboard software allows you to save text-marking features to respond to in a later lesson.

The training materials available for schools (DfES 2004) present an example of shared reading in a year 1 class using an electronic version of a big book from the website www.naturegrid.org.uk. The big books on this website have been designed to be used within the literacy hour. They include many of the NLS keywords. Photographs and moving graphics and sounds are accompanied by simple text with questions to help children interpret what they see. The interactivity and the high-quality photographic images provide variety and interest.

FIGURE 3.1 An example of an electronic book

The second type of texts are electronic texts which are non-linear and are read in a quite different way from traditional texts. They include CD-Rom encyclopaedias and internet pages and tend to be non-fiction texts which involve particular skills in locating, identifying and extracting information. These kinds of texts are layered and contain hypertext links and moving images. Electronic texts are redefining literacy by introducing new ways of reading and writing and pupils need a different set of reading skills to navigate ICT texts successfully. These skills can be modelled during shared reading sessions. An example, again from NLS materials (DfES 2001), is that of a Year 6 class using an ICT suite for shared reading. A factual ICT text from a website on the local environment is used and the pupils focus on summarising and then making notes on a text. The context is a local studies project on Solihull currently being undertaken by this particular class. The teacher is able to draw the children's attention to the key points of information in the article and all pupils can be involved by text marking the most important points.

The shared reading leads into shared writing as the teacher demonstrates how to make notes. A split screen is used with the ICT text and a word-processor open simultaneously. The children are shown how ICT can support the note-making process. Sections of the original text are highlighted and dragged into a word-processor, removing the need for tedious rewriting and allowing concentration on the reasons for making particular selections. A similar type of text could be used for researching a topic to provide material for a brochure or leaflet or to research the background to a text. At the simplest level young children can be shown how to find out more about a topic of interest ranging from information about healthy eating to facts about sport or animal lives.

A broader definition of shared reading can also include responding to film, television and audio recordings. Research evidence about ICT and English notes the importance of teachers' understanding of visual literacy (Goodwyn *et al.* 1997; Reid *et al.* 2002). Teachers need to be aware of the link between visual or cine-literacy and the more traditional skills of print literacy. An example from speaking and listening guidance (DfES 2003b) focuses on identifying the main sections of a piece of film or video and how these are signalled through voice-over, music and graphics. In this example, children watch the opening sequence of two extracts from children's broadcasts. They are questioned about how the content of the film is signalled and encouraged to use appropriate terminology. Points are made about how news broadcasts would be introduced by different types of music compared to narratives or cartoons. In a further whole class teaching situation the children watch longer broadcasts and discuss presentational features – for example, captions, charts, stills, animation and the use of music at different points in the broadcast. The advice given in this guidance material is general, but very specific guidance is given on using films with children in a publication from the British Film Institute (BFI 2004).

Shared writing

The principle of shared writing is one of whole class teaching in which the teacher 'scaffolds' the children's learning by modelling writing skills and strategies (Washtell 1998). Scaffolding refers to a process which enables pupils to solve a problem or task which would be beyond their unassisted efforts. The technique of shared writing is described and expanded on in two publications: *Grammar for Writing* (DfEE 2000) and *Developing Early Writing* (DfES 2001b). Shared writing has been promoted by the NLS as an effective method for teaching writing:

> Teachers should…compose texts, teaching how they are planned and how ideas are sequenced, clarified and structured.
>
> (DfEE 1998: 11)

ICT can contribute greatly to a teacher's ability to model writing processes. Writing can easily be changed, improved, reworked and represented using a word-processor and this can be demonstrated and the provisional nature of written information can be emphasised.

This case study is taken from Tyldesley (2002). A year 1 teacher aimed to provide support with early writing skills. The shared text she was using was a big book version of a 'patterned' story.

Once upon a time an old man planted a turnip seed.

The turnip grew and grew and grew.

At the end of the story they all shared the turnip.

FIGURE 3.2 An example of a sequencing activity based on a patterned story

The literacy objective was to enable pupils to sequence and retell an existing text. A program was used which enables objects to be easily picked up, dropped and dragged (My World). The children suggested which incidents should be chosen and the screen was set up in front of the children. Text snippets became 'objects' enabling children to sequence key incidents from the text. Focused discussion enabled learning to take place. The activity took place in whole class teaching time; the teacher could model and the children could participate. Groups then completed the activity independently. More able groups were able to use text-entering facilities to extend the description of the key incidents. The activity was embedded into general class work as some of the groups were able to do the same activity cutting and sequencing sentences on paper.

The use of the word-processor made the children more aware of the patterned and repetitive nature of the original. It also supported fast and professional 'publishing'. Writing was given a clear purpose and two class books were produced that could be compared and reread alongside the original text.

Young children find independent writing a laborious process. Word-processors can be set up as writing frames with some text which cannot be altered and text boxes in which new words can be added. Children can then 'innovate' on an original text with a minimal need to enter text. One of the difficulties with using a

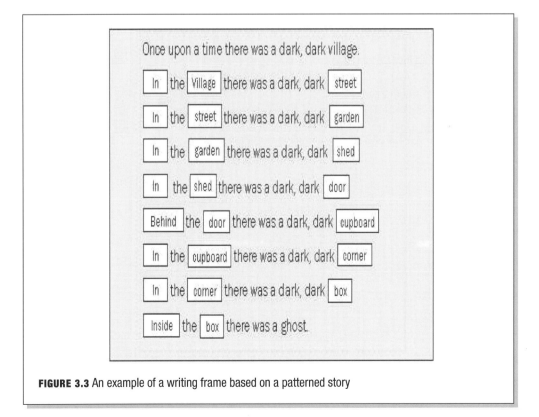

FIGURE 3.3 An example of a writing frame based on a patterned story

word-processor with young children is the length of time needed to complete a word-processing task. Writing frames allow texts to be quickly created with the same patterned structure as the original.

The next example with year 3 pupils (Tyldesley 2002) demonstrates the importance of modelling the provisional nature of text and how word-processed texts can be manipulated on screen. In shared reading the class read various poems and discussed rhyme, rhythm and structure. A poem about colours was used as a model for writing. The teacher demonstrated using the structure of the poem as a basis for creating new verse. She also made an interesting use of the 'word list' facility on the word-processor. A list of rhyming words was brainstormed by the class and typed into the word-processor. This was quickly transferred into a 'word list' becoming a customised list of vocabulary for pupils to insert into their writing. The list was used as a support by children writing on paper and those word-processing. The list appears on the word-processing page and speech feedback can be set so that pupils can hear the words read out loud and insert them into their writing.

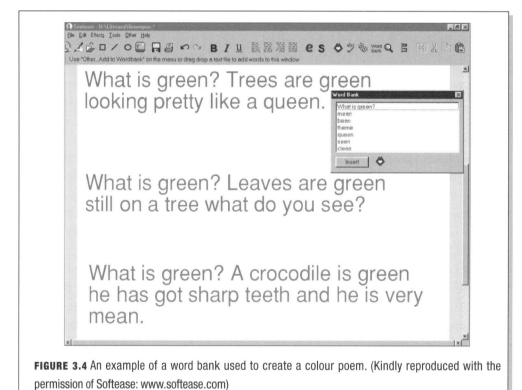

FIGURE 3.4 An example of a word bank used to create a colour poem. (Kindly reproduced with the permission of Softease: www.softease.com)

The key change for this teacher was using a computer as a tool for whole class demonstration. She reported pupils' view of writing shifting as a result of more wholescale changes being made to an existing text. The provisional nature of text on a word-processor made children aware that words are not like 'bricks in a wall' that cannot be moved or changed.

The provisional nature of ICT texts is significant. Another important aspect of ICT as a tool to teach writing is the new dimension created in terms of different audiences and purposes for writing. Some possibilities include:

- Communicating with real and fictional people via fax, email, webchat, and so on
- Reading and contributing to online stories
- Creating web pages to communicate information and ideas

(Bennett 2004: 47)

These possibilities will be discussed in more detail in Chapter 5. However, whole class teaching provides an opportunity to model purposeful communication in which the purpose and audience of the writing is made explicit and meaningful.

This final example is of whole class shared writing using ICT with key stage 2 pupils. The theme was persuasive writing and the focus of the writing was to persuade parents that it would be a good idea to introduce a new pet into the family. The computer was used as a shared writing tool with all the pupils grouped round the screen. A writing frame was already loaded. The children suggested which sentences might be entered using the plan drawn up on the previous day. The teacher acted as a scribe and children came up and typed in their suggestions. The emphasis was on a draft copy so that spelling and punctuation did not interfere with the flow of ideas. Being able to insert, delete and modify the text as they went along enhanced the shared writing session (see Figure 3.5 on p. 40).

During independent work the lowest achieving group sequenced sentences they had encountered previously. Sentences had been entered on a program that enabled them to click, move and drop pieces of text. They had the help of a teaching assistant to read and remind them of the structure of persuasive writing. They were not hampered by handwriting and spelling difficulties and could concentrate on the sense and sequence of the text.

One group used the writing frame demonstrated during shared writing to help them structure their persuasive writing. The two most able groups produced their own persuasive text. Phrases in an 'on screen' word list were used for support but did not have to be used. Speech feedback enabled appropriate choices to be made.

Whole class word and sentence level teaching

The third aspect of whole class teaching is word and sentence level work using the objectives focused on spelling, phonics and grammar from the NLS Framework. Word level work often includes interactive activities such as those promoted by *Progression in Phonics* for key stage 1 (DfEE 1999) and *Grammar for Writing* in key stage 2 (DfEE 2000). Many of these activities can be enriched by the use of ICT.

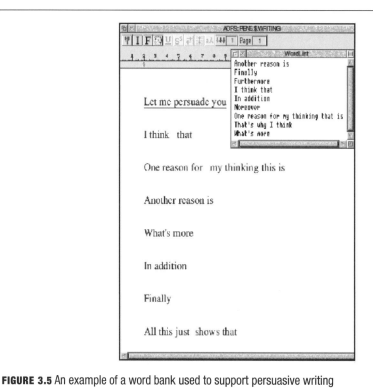

FIGURE 3.5 An example of a word bank used to support persuasive writing

ICT can be a useful tool when investigating spelling conventions or punctuation rules. For example, a passage from a text discussed in shared reading can be word-processed and presented to the whole class. Different word classes can be highlighted, for example all verbs could be highlighted in red. This generates a great deal of discussion as most texts contain a number of verbs in different forms such as infinitives 'to sing', past tense forms such as 'was', 'came', and so on and present participles such as 'thumping', 'spreading', 'panting'.

Phonics teaching can be supported by ICT. During phonics whole class teaching, prepared lists of words can be segmented into their constituent phonemes. This can be demonstrated on an interactive whiteboard or overhead projector. Children can then be asked to take part and sort words into different phoneme groups. For example, words with the /er/ phoneme spelt 'er', 'ur' or 'ir' can be sorted. Many word-processors have a drag-and-drop facility, making this kind of investigation quick and easy. Presentation software has features which enable word chunks to move across the screen. These dynamic facilities make explanations clearer and help focus pupils' attention. The speech feedback can also be used so that pupils can check that they are not just choosing words for their visual pattern. Pupils benefit from the interactivity of speech feedback and their selections can be confirmed or rejected as a result of this feedback.

Investigations with lists of roots and suffixes are also possible. A word-processor will highlight wrongly spelt words – for example, 'beautifull' – so that children have their attention drawn to errors and can work out rules more easily for themselves.

Relevant research and inspection evidence

Moseley *et al.* (1999) conducted research into effective pedagogy with ICT. The focus was on literacy and ICT teaching in primary schools. One finding was that much computer use in the classroom was planned as an addition rather than as a key teaching strategy. One implication of the research was that using ICT for direct instruction in some cases would be appropriate. Presentation software enables teachers to show ideas dynamically, for example when showing suffixes joining with root words.

A case study from *Ways Forward with ICT* (Moseley *et al.* 1999)

Year 2 pupils developed an extended piece of writing following whole class teaching presented with presentation software. The teacher used this software to help the pupils identify the appropriate common spelling patterns for vowel phonemes in texts, as well as to teach specific word endings and for some word level revision work. To do this she used slides to present stories. At the end of these presentations she added some extra slides to revise word level work. The feature of the program which enabled the teacher to present word level endings, such as 'ing' or 'ed', by having them move across the screen was particularly helpful in focusing pupils' attention. After the initial teaching, the pupils used a word-processor with speech facility and an on-screen word grid and put into practice some of the word level learning. The talking word-processor read a passage and the pupils were able to identify words which the computer could not read properly. They also decided where they thought punctuation should be placed in a prepared passage from the text. The teacher was able to use presentation software effectively and make appropriate decisions about when to use ICT as part of her broader literacy teaching.

Creative uses of ICT in whole class teaching

Fulfilling the Potential: Transforming Teaching and Learning through ICT in Schools (DfES 2003c) discusses transforming teaching and learning through ICT. The paper makes the point that nearly all schools are connected to the internet and that ICT resources have recently been greatly improved, yet the vast majority of schools do not tap into the transformational potential of ICT. To practitioners, the government's view of transformation can seem out of reach and removed from classroom realities. Being 'creative' appears to be more accessible than 'transformation'. Yet what do we mean by creativity in the primary classroom? Creativity is surely about capturing pupils' imagination and engaging pupils in a broad and rich curriculum. In a further publication, *Excellence and Enjoyment* (DfES 2003a), the government has recognised the importance of the enjoyment of learning and the benefits of creative learning. The document notes that, 'The best primary schools have developed timetables and teaching plans that combine creativity and strong teaching in the basics' (DfES 2003a: 18).

However, some educationalists (for example, Wyse and Jones 2004) are critical of the government's approach and argue that it is impossible to be creative with the straitjacket of the NLS Framework still in place. They argue that this is too prescriptive and that it is the implementation of the NLS that is hindering creativity. So how do we balance these different views and establish creative ways of engaging in whole class teaching with ICT? A creative approach in whole class teaching may include the following:

- Willingness to take risks
- Emphasis on problem-solving and an enquiry-based approach to learning
- Recognition of the need to take into account preferred learning styles
- Enrichment of learning by first-hand experience

Many of the above points are taken into account in the examples in this chapter. Often, using more complex ICT tools involves taking more risks; ICT can involve more interaction, higher quality visual resources and excellent material based on real-life situations. It also often gives teachers more choice of materials and teaching strategies in whole class teaching situations.

Inclusion and support for learning

During both shared reading and writing it is important to respond to the range of different needs within a particular group of pupils. ICT tools can often provide support for learning for pupils with difficulties and a greater degree of challenge for all pupils. Teaching resources can be found on the internet which motivate, provide variety and stimulate a range of pupils. Differentiated texts and activities can also be saved and then modified, for example by simplifying the text, increasing visual support, reducing the content or increasing the point size. This can also provide variety for pupils with a range of learning styles. Pupils with English as an Additional Language can be supported by providing more visual prompts from ICT sources, for example, internet sites and clip art. However, there is a danger that whole class teaching using ICT can provide material for visual learners but little for kinaesthetic learners. Traditional transmission teaching can also be disguised with a new technology, such as interactive whiteboards, and yet their use may be far from interactive. An important point is made in a Becta smartboard evaluation, 'the whiteboard needs to be in the class and used by the children as well as the teacher' (Smith 2001).

Future developments

ICT is likely to continue to be an intrinsic element of whole class literacy teaching. However, it is important that teachers continue to develop and exploit the creative potential of ICT rather than focusing on simple presentational tools. The future could see the possibility of all pupils able to access material electronically at any time from a wide range of sources and able to communicate instantly with a wide range of audiences. This has implications for the role of whole class teaching and the relationship between the learner and teacher. Children will have much more access to information and the teacher may need to respond to rather than initiate the learning process. The traditional definition of literacy will continue to expand with electronic texts and electronic communication being used ever more widely. The teacher's role will need to accommodate these changes with whole class teaching used as a flexible and responsive teaching strategy.

Web links

http://www.literacytrust.org.uk/Research/ICTindex.html – this literacy site includes a research page with links to research summaries on ICT and English.

http://www.filmeducation.org – useful film clips are available from this site.

http://www.bfi.org.uk – this site has useful information on using film in primary schools and contains film video clips and lesson plans to use in literacy teaching.

http://www.naturegrid.org.uk/infant/index.html – an environmental site with electronic big books and ideas for cross-curricular literacy teaching in key stage 1.

http://www.storiesfromtheweb.org/index.htm – an online resource of stories, poems, pupils' work and word games suitable for key stage 2.

http://www.kented.org.uk/ngfl/subjects/literacy/Writing-frames – this is a downloadable resource in Word format, of a selection of writing frames.

References

Bennett, R. (2004) *Using ICT in Primary English Teaching*. Exeter: Learning Matters.

BFI/DfES (2004) *Look Again: A Teaching Guide to Using Film and Television with Three to Eleven Year Olds*. London: DfES/BFI.

DfEE (1998) *National Literacy Strategy Framework*. London: DfEE.

DfEE (1999) *Progression in Phonics*. London: DfEE.

DfEE/QCA (1999) *The National Curriculum Handbook for Primary Teachers in England*. London: DfEE/QCA.

DfEE (2000) *Grammar for Writing*. London: DfEE.

DES (1992) *Curriculum Organisation and Classroom Practice in Primary Schools*. London: DES.

DfES (2001a) *ICT in the Literacy hour: Whole Class Teaching*. London: DfES.

DfES (2001b) *Developing Early Writing*. London: DfES.

DfES (2003a) *Excellence and Enjoyment*. London: DfES.

DfES (2003b) *Speaking, Listening and Learning: Working with Children in Key Stages 1 and 2*. London: DfES.

DfES (2003c) *Fulfilling the Potential: Transforming Teaching and Learning through ICT in Schools*. London: DfES.

DfES (2004) *Learning and Teaching using ICT*. London: DfES.

English, E., Hargreaves, L. and Hislam, J. (2002) 'Pedagogical dilemmas in the National Literacy Strategy: primary teachers' perceptions, reflections and classroom behaviour.' *Cambridge Journal of Education*, 32, 1, pp. 9–26.

Goodwyn, A. *et al.* (1997) 'The future Curriculum in English and IT: how teachers and student teachers view the relationship.' *Journal of Information Technology for Teacher Education*, 6, 3 pp. 227–40.

Holdaway, D. (1979) *The Foundations of Literacy*. Sydney: Ashton Scholastic.

MAPE (1998) *MAPE Focus on Literacy Pack*. Northampton: MAPE Publications.

Moseley, D. and Higgins, S. (1999) *Ways Forward with ICT: Effective Pedagogy using Information and Communications Technology for Literacy and Numeracy in Primary Schools*. Newcastle: University of Newcastle.

Reid, M. *et al.* (2002) *Evaluation Report of the Becta Digital Video Pilot Project*. Coventry: Becta.

Smith, H. (2001) 'Smartboard evaluation: final report' www.kented.org.uk/ngfl/whiteboards (accessed 28.07.04).

Tyldesley, A. (2002) 'A reflective view of the NLS', in *Teaching Primary Literacy with ICT*. Monteith, M. (ed.) Buckingham: Open University Press.

Washtell, A. (1998) 'Routines and resources' in *Writing Under Control: Teaching Writing in the Primary School*, Graham, J. and Kelly, A. London: David Fulton.

Wyse, D. and Jones, R. (eds) (2004) *Creativity in the Primary Curriculum*. London: David Fulton.

4

Guided and independent work with ICT

Chapter overview

Teachers and trainee teachers may wonder about the best way of integrating ICT into the independent and guided section of the literacy hour or literacy session. Guided work and independent work were set out by the national literacy strategy (NLS) framework (DfEE 1998) as essential elements of literacy teaching offering focused group teaching and the opportunity to develop independent working skills and habits. However, ICT has not always taken a prominent role in these guided or independent sessions. It is relatively uncommon for electronic books and interactive texts to be used for guided reading or for teachers to support guided writing using word-processors. This chapter will consider how ICT texts can be used effectively during guided reading and how guided writing activities using ICT can be supported.

Introduction

Guided work is an area of uncertainty for some teachers and this chapter will provide extra information and guidance. Independent literacy work is also often a cause for concern for teachers. Differentiated activities need to be planned which meet pupils' needs and can be carried out without direct adult intervention. ICT can help provide support through particular word-processing facilities such as word banks and on screen grids. These can be customised to meet the needs of particular pupils. Teachers and assistants can prepare banks of relevant words and phrases to be used in independent writing. Similarly, writing frames can be provided which give a structure for children's work, for example introducing phrases that link one paragraph to the next.

Differentiation and inclusion issues are particularly relevant in this chapter and so is the role of other adults in supporting learning. Teaching assistants and all adults involved with learning in the classroom can take a significant role in guided work and can support pupils working more independently. It can be crucial to have extra adult support if guided work is being led by the class teacher. A teaching assistant often has a very specific role with a particular group and can of course support the use of ICT. The role of extra adults does have to be planned very carefully so that children continue to develop independent working habits, but there is also someone on hand to provide reassurance and sometimes technical support if necessary.

As before, this chapter will take note of research and inspection evidence and make links to guidance and statutory documentation, such as the NLS framework and other material from the government on guided work. The case studies should also help to provide ideas about relevant guided and independent activities using ICT. Every child's literacy skills should include the ability to read and write in the ICT medium and the integration of ICT, particularly into guided and independent work, can play a significant part in developing these skills and abilities.

Using ICT in guided work

It is useful to consider the range of ways ICT might be used in a guided session. The ideas that follow provide a range of ways of integrating ICT into guided work. For example, as an introduction to using electronic texts more independently, a teacher might use ICT to introduce a particular electronic text such as a CD-Rom or even a website that the children will need to learn to access and explore. Guided work may also be used to demonstrate a specific piece of software as long as this will provide opportunities for more independent involvement. The teacher may decide that a small group situation is more beneficial for this demonstration because the software will only be used with certain pupils to either support or challenge their learning. There may also be occasions when it is relevant to access and demonstrate particular interactive texts such as talking books, branching stories and adventure programs. The complex choices involved may need discussion and demonstration so that pupils can use the texts to their full potential. Guided work can also provide the opportunity for individual and small group support with word-processing tasks that would otherwise be too challenging.

Hardware considerations

In order to facilitate guided work, it is helpful to consider what kind of hardware would be most useful. A small cluster of computers, for example, would be acceptable for any type of guided work; alternatives might be a set of portable computers or laptops. However, it is well worth considering organising some sessions to take place in a computer suite. In this case the teacher could guide the work of one group while other pupils worked independently on computers, perhaps supported by a teaching assistant. A single computer is not really satisfactory for guided work as pupils are unlikely to have enough access to the text to gain more independent skills. This focus on guided work creating a bridge from teacher-directed activities to independence is discussed more fully in the next section of the chapter. However, it can be beneficial for pupils to work in pairs within the group situation. This would allow discussion and interaction and also would mean that for a group of six pupils only three desk top machines or laptops would be needed.

A background to guided and independent work and the national literacy strategy

For many years teachers have chosen to group children for reading and writing activities. Guided work was formalised as a result of the inclusion of guided reading and writing in the structure of the literacy hour (DfEE 1998). Guided work differs from some more informal arrangements because of the presence of the teacher and the organisation of children into differentiated groups (Graham and Kelly 2000). The theory behind guided work in the NLS was that it provided a bridge between whole class teaching in which children have a more dependent role and the expectation that they will be able to work in a fully independent situation. The teacher or assistant 'guides' but does not over-direct and gives children the opportunity to move towards independence. However, guided reading does tend to cover a multitude of different practices. Similarly, guided writing is carried out but schools often do not have a clear sense of what is involved.

Guided reading and writing have been included in the intervention programmes for children experiencing difficulties in literacy. These programmes are carried out by teaching assistants who now have considerable skills in teaching guided reading and writing. The rationale for guided work in the NLS framework is to enable the teacher to teach at least one group per day and to enable pupils to work independently (DfEE 1998). Guided work can also, of course, be carried out by trained teaching assistants. This is in line with the NLS intention to promote more direct teaching of literacy and in the process improve literacy standards.

Guided reading

Guided reading was a strategy used by the First Steps programme in Western Australia (Dewsbury 1999) and in New Zealand in the 1980s, but before the National Literacy Strategy it was not widely used in UK schools. The previous practice of hearing individual children read was heavily criticised by Ofsted (DES 1992) as inefficient and time-consuming for the teacher and unproductive for the children and was seen as practising skills rather than developing strategies. In guided reading, the teacher works with a group of pupils around the same ability level, which is seen to be more efficient in terms of time. The pupils read individually from multiple copies of the same text. Learning objectives are selected to provide support with a specific aspect of reading. Texts can cover a range and should be challenging but possible for the children to read independently. The range of texts can include fiction, non-fiction and ICT texts although it is still relatively rare for ICT texts to be used in this kind of group teaching situation.

Some experts see the role of the teacher within a guided reading session as someone who intervenes where necessary if the pupils are in danger of losing meaning. Makgill (1999) uses the phrase 'flying solo under supervision' to describe this process. Most experts, however, agree that guided reading is planned and focused instruction in reading conducted in small group settings. Hobsbaum (2003) notes that the teacher is acting as the expert who guides the learners through the text, by providing signposts to the most important and most helpful features of the textual landscape. The emphasis is on guidance and the ultimate goal is to foster independent reading.

Teachers have themselves needed some guidance with this teaching technique and there are two excellent resources available: *Book Bands for Guided Reading* is a helpful resource for children reading at the early model (Bickler 2003); for transitional and fluent readers, *Guided Reading at key stage 2* (Hobsbaum 2003) gives some good examples of texts and how they might be used. However, neither resource considers electronic texts in any detail.

Guided reading with ICT texts

ICT texts are often particularly challenging texts for children to access and the structured nature of a guided session can enable greater support and instruction to take place. The view of the NLS is that:

> The occasional use of an electronic text rather than a book can significantly expand children's reading experience. It can also provide a medium for learning and applying important new reading skills.
>
> (DfES 2003b)

The reasons for using ICT texts in guided reading are to provide some focused teaching on developing and applying the skills needed to access these non-linear, interactive and multimedia texts as well as developing reading skills in a different context. There are two main categories of texts, as discussed in Chapter 3: electronic versions of 'real books' with some added interactive features and genuine ICT texts, usually written in an electronic format which cannot be fully represented in paper form.

Selecting ICT texts for guided reading

It is rare to find fully interactive fiction texts apart from some multiple choice adventures and some electronic versions of paper texts. Non-fiction texts are likely to be the main choice for guided reading sessions. Examples include:

- CD-Roms
- Websites
- TV text services

Children need support to access and interact with aspects of ICT texts including the following features:

- Non-linear layout
- Interactive features
- Interlinked pages
- Dynamic presentation
- Multimedia features

It should be possible to find interactive ICT texts for all the main non-fiction text types listed in the NLS Framework and the National Curriculum. These texts would then provide opportunities to teach the NLS text level objectives for non-fiction for a particular year and term. The texts are likely to include a range of functions and styles, for example, websites may include the following range (DfES 2003b):

- News and update sites
- Information sites
- Shopping and booking sites
- General interest sites
- Utility sites
- Sites designed for children

As with any guided reading text, an appropriate choice must be made for a particular group bearing in mind their particular needs. The text must be accessible in style and content and at an instructional reading level. It is always important to choose good quality texts and good examples of the text type, although examples do often cover more than one type.

When using ICT texts, the aim of the sessions would usually involve the following:

- Exploring specific reading and response issues relating to any non-linear, interactive, multimedia, interlinked or dynamic features
- Focusing on particular reading strategies needed to engage effectively with these texts (DfES 2003b)

The structure of guided reading

Guided reading teaching is divided by the NLS Framework (DfEE 1998) into the following sections:

- Text introduction
- Strategy check
- Independent reading
- Return to the text, and
- Response to reading

The aim of each section of the guided reading session is to encourage students to think and talk about the text as it is read.

Text introduction

A text introduction is crucial to anticipate challenges for the early reader but this becomes less significant for more fluent readers who may predict and generate questions prior to reading. As far as ICT texts are concerned, a text introduction can focus on a discussion of where this type of text is usually encountered and how it is usually accessed. Other discussion points could include:

- Previous experience with this type of text
- Purpose of the text and what it can offer to the reader
- How the content, style and vocabulary relate to the ICT features

Strategy check

The NLS encourages a strategy check which enables early readers to articulate the strategies they will use when they come across unknown words. A strategy check is also useful with ICT texts to ensure children know how to solve problems or how to make critical judgements about the author's intention. Focus points can include:

- How to navigate in order to find information
- How the reading approach differs from traditional texts
- How to select appropriate information

Independent reading

The idea of guided reading is that children read independently and at their own pace. In the case of ICT texts the children would read on screen. Teachers had many concerns when this method was first introduced as they were not required to listen to every word during a reading session. However, if the text is matched closely to a child's ability, the teacher does not have to be so closely involved. Their role is to intervene to solve problems rather than to listen to reading and, in the case of ICT texts, to capitalise on the specific opportunities and demands these texts provide. The purpose for reading and the outcomes would relate to this ICT format. The teacher can provide prompts for discussion and can scaffold the session so that children make progress with a search for meaning and an ability to interrogate texts.

Return to the text

Following on from independent reading is a return to the text and a chance to highlight strategies used to solve difficulties. The teacher needs to encourage an exploration of what has been learnt that might be different from using a paper based text. It is also useful to lead reflection on how and when particular ICT reading strategies were used.

Response to the text

Response could include evaluation of the effectiveness and usefulness of this text compared to other ICT texts and compared to paper texts. The teacher could also elicit children's personal response to the experience of reading ICT texts.

Guided reading case studies

We will now consider two case studies of guided reading with ICT texts. The first case study is taken from NLS guidance material on guided reading (DfES 2003b). The example is of a guided reading session with year 2 children reading from screens on laptops around one table while other pupils work independently. The text is an electronic dictionary. The second example of guided reading using an ICT text is taken from Hobsbaum (2003). This example is based around the use of a CD-Rom encyclopaedia with year 5 pupils.

Case study

Text introduction

The teacher supported exploration of the features of the electronic dictionary building on the children's understanding. She gave short activities and asked the children to report back on various definitions. The focus was on the ICT skills and strategies needed compared with those used with a paper-based dictionary.

Strategy check

The strategy check was used to focus on a particular feature of the dictionary, which is the facility to split polysyllabic words. The children were encouraged to discuss this reading strategy.

Independent reading

The teacher demonstrated the reading task, which was to find similar words to the keywords accessed previously. The aim was to enrich vocabulary and to develop particular ICT skills. The group read independently while the teacher worked with each child in turn and reminded them of the reading strategies discussed earlier.

Return to the text

The group discussed their reading and the outcome of the task, including how and where they found particular words. The teacher prompted discussion of the strategies used.

Response to the text

The session concluded with comparisons and evaluations of electronic dictionaries as opposed to paper-based versions. The children evaluated the advantages and disadvantages and started to state reasons for their preferences.

Case study

Text introduction

The teacher gathered the group around the computer monitor with an electronic encyclopaedia (Encarta) pre-loaded. She encouraged the children to discuss the home page and the information that was available in each section. The teacher demonstrated how to efficiently locate an article on the subject of volcanoes.

Strategy check

She reminded pupils about how to scan for specific information using a keyword (for example, 'active') and then note or mark the relevant information.

Independent reading

The focus for independent reading was to scan for relevant information and make notes. The task was to note down five recently active volcanoes and the last time they were active. The children were given a table for recording. The pupils worked with their own copy of the text on screen. Hobsbaum (2003) stresses the role of the teacher in observing, prompting and praising each child in turn while focusing on pupils' scanning and note-making strategies.

Return to the text

Pupils shared their findings when they gathered together as a group. The teacher generated a discussion of efficient scanning techniques.

Response to the text

Pupils were encouraged to discuss the advantages and disadvantages of electronic reference sources compared to paper-based sources and to state their preferences.

Guided writing

The NLS describes guided writing as a strategy in which the teacher works with a specific ability group to support them in applying principles they have learnt in shared sessions (DfEE 1999). Beard (2000) claims that guided writing is effective because it tackles problems in a spirit of shared inquiry and problem-solving. However, despite the fact that guided writing has been part of the NLS since its inception in 1998, teachers have been unclear as to what guided writing teaching sessions should consist of. An HMI report commented that teachers often sit with a group but do not engage children in sustained teaching or they over-direct the work (HMI 2000).

The actual intention of guided writing is to provide an additional supported step towards independent writing. Children find it difficult to move from whole class instruction to writing independently. During children's independent writing sessions teachers are often not involved in specific teaching. They may observe, monitor and provide support with transcriptional aspects, for example providing help with spelling. Guided writing, on the other hand, provides an opportunity for a teacher to focus on a group that needs specific support or challenge with particular objectives. During this group session the children should be actively involved in composing and revising their own texts, supported by the teacher. In guided work the teacher supports and scaffolds rather than leading and directing. Within this context, Medwell *et al.* (2002) suggest three main purposes for guided writing:

1   To help children plan and draft their independent work

2   To help children revise and edit work they have already begun

3   To provide differentiated support for particular children or groups (Medwell *et al.* 2002 107–8)

The NLS (DfEE 1999) also suggest that guided writing sessions should be organised into the following categories: guided writing sessions *before* writing, guided writing sessions *during* the writing process, guided writing sessions *after* writing. A suggested structure is provided for each of these sessions which has some links to the structure of a guided reading session. Guided writing *during* the writing process is particularly emphasised by the NLS as the key type of guided writing. The suggested structure is as follows:

- Review
- Cue in
- Try, improve, share, appraise
- Recapitulate

This structure consists of an introduction, time for independent writing and a return to the group for a discussion of key learning points. The aim of the introduction is to focus on the purpose of the task, make links to reading and discuss text features. The middle section focuses on ongoing editing and improvement of writing and 'oral rehearsal', a term which means trying out written phrases before committing them to paper. The final session enables review and evaluation. The structure works well with a short defined non-fiction text type or a short passage of writing but fits less well with writing a more sustained piece.

Guided writing sessions using ICT could focus profitably on some of the structures outlined above. Using a word-processor has often been seen as an isolated independent activity for an individual or small group to complete in the classroom setting. Often, children have not been supported in using the full facilities of word-processing and in extreme cases the computer has been used merely as a presentational tool. A planned guided writing session enables a teacher or teaching assistant to focus on a particular stage of the writing process and to ensure that word-processors are used to their full potential.

Guided writing case studies

We shall now consider three case studies – one using laptops, one using palmtops and one using the Clicker program.

Case study

Guided writing sessions will often be strongly linked to reading sessions. In this first example of guided writing teaching with year 4 pupils, the children accessed information from a website and learnt how to take effective notes. Note taking is one of the most difficult topics to teach effectively. More specific group support is often necessary to challenge pupils to identify and extract information from texts. An effective method of note taking with electronic texts is to use cut-and-paste techniques. A split screen can be very useful as the original text can be open alongside a blank word-processing page.

In this particular case a teacher worked with a small group of year 4 pupils to support note taking. A bank of wireless laptops was used and each child had access to a website page of information about space. The teacher supported the pupils in creating a split screen with the website page on one side and a word-processing page on the other. This had been demonstrated previously in a shared session. The purpose of the note making was to organise and summarise the content, abbreviate ideas and select key words. The aim was also to develop greater understanding of the material.

Guided writing enabled the teacher to work with the group while they actually made decisions about keywords in each paragraph and then ensured that they were able to successfully paste these words and phrases into a word-processor and create summarised bullet points which gave key facts about space. The children later used a paint package to illustrate their note taking.

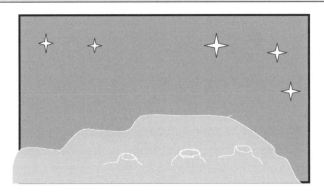

The Moon

Key Facts

* The moon is lit by the sun.
* Sometimes the moon is invisible.
* It changes shape every 29 days.

* As wide as Australia.
* 384,400 km from Earth.
* No atmosphere.
* Astronauts landed 1969.
* It can be as hot as 100c.

FIGURE 4.1 An example of writing produced as a result of guided writing

Case study

The second guided writing example is taken from *Ways Forward with ICT* (Moseley and Higgins 1999). The focus was on using palmtops with year 3 and year 4 to revise and redraft work. The teacher believed that these computers were particularly valuable as tools to teach redrafting and the use of the spell checker and thesaurus, and they were used for short non-narrative texts and poetry writing. These short tasks avoided the limitation of the small screen which can interfere with the coherence of longer pieces of writing.

The pupils preferred reviewing printouts of their writing and appeared to make more critical evaluations of written work away from the screen. Although the research project does not go into detail about how editing was encouraged guided writing does provide a useful forum for discussing editing with a group and allowing peer discussion of points for improvement and detection of errors.

The project found that palmtops were most useful in facilitating revising, redrafting and editing and that initial planning and drafting were best done by hand, at least until pupils became competent at keyboard skills. The palmtops were especially useful for producing a weekly news sheet, which was reorganised, revised and edited. Guided writing is a teaching technique which can be particularly useful to encourage a greater degree of improvement and polish to finished pieces of writing.

Case study

The third example of guided writing is with much younger pupils. These pupils were based in a foundation stage setting and needed encouragement to move to independent writing. They used a bank of computers with the program Clicker (Crick software). The teacher set up this program with a pre-prepared grid using key words and phrases to support the children in writing a simple account. Prepared word banks or grids provide scaffolded support but the presence of a teacher or teaching assistant can lead to more independent choice of vocabulary and encourage the use of editing tools. In this case the teacher wanted the children to write an account of a recent visit to a city farm. They used the repeated phrase 'we saw' and chose appropriate words and phrases (supported by pictures) to list animals and objects seen on the visit.

Independent work using ICT

We have discussed how ICT can contribute to guided reading and writing activities. The NLS also wish to promote the contribution ICT can make to children's independent work during literacy teaching. In Chapter 3 the rationale for the literacy hour was discussed and some of the consequences noted. Teachers have found it hard to balance the demands of the literacy hour with ICT use. As stated previously, ICT use was largely neglected in the early stages of the NLS implementation. However, with additional resources it should be possible for ICT to make an important contribution to children's independent work during literacy teaching and during the literacy hour.

NLS guidance on ICT (DfES 2003b) notes that ICT activities need to contribute to cohesion within the literacy hour. The point being made is that ICT activities are much more relevant if they are fully related to the main teaching points of the lesson rather than, as sometimes happens, 'bolt on' activities unrelated to the main objectives. It can sometimes happen that all pupils follow up what has been taught apart from pupils using a computer.

The focus for literacy learning, according to the NLS, should always be the objectives at text, sentence and word level. ICT can of course provide a meaningful context for discussion and collaboration around these objectives. The power of ICT to motivate and engage has been noted by many teachers. It can also support differentiation both by giving access to the curriculum for pupils with SEN and by providing further challenges for more able pupils. ICT can also help relate literacy learning to the wider curriculum and to the 'real world'.

To summarise, ICT can support text, sentence and word level objectives during independent literacy work by providing:

- Access to electronic texts and interactive ICT texts which cannot exist on paper
- A tool for writing and developing writing
- Various supports and scaffolding for writing
- A way of presenting and publishing writing
- A purpose and outcome for writing
- A context for word and sentence level investigation and exploration (DfES 2003b)

The following sections give further examples of using ICT in independent work time.

Accessing electronic and interactive ICT texts

Print texts can be loaded or scanned into the computer. These texts can then be moved, changed, highlighted and annotated or cut and pasted into other documents. ICT texts which are often interactive, non-linear and dynamic are also an important source of information and research.

Tools for writing and developing writing

A variety of word-processing packages is available, which allow text to be manipulated, edited stored and retrieved. Word-processing is particularly important for children's conceptualisation of the writing process. If you use word-processors to their full capacity, you become aware that writing is a dynamic and developmental process. However, word-processing does need appropriate teaching that, according to the NLS, should take place outside the literacy hour.

A key principle is also the importance of composing directly onto the screen rather than using a word-processor to 'copy up' completed work. Many teachers reported in the literature are only using word-processing for pupils to present their work even though the greatest potential is for pupils to compose, draft, revise and organise their thinking and writing (Becta 2003). Research has also found that the writing process is more collaborative, iterative and social in computer classrooms as compared to paper-and-pencil environments (Goldberg *et al.* 2003).

Supports and scaffolds for writing

ICT can provide many supports which help children to make progress with the stages of writing development. Examples include:

- Electronic writing frames
- Text, picture or audio prompts – a program like Clicker provides these prompts
- General or customised word, phrase or sentence banks
- Spelling and grammar checking facilities
- On-screen dictionaries and thesaurus

A purpose and outcome for writing

Providing a motivating purpose for writing is often an issue in the classroom. ICT can provide both a purpose and an outcome for writing that is not necessarily paper based. Examples include:

- Email
- A web page
- A multimedia presentation
- An electronic database

These are all important means of communication in many situations. Research shows that pupils who write for a real audience using the internet or email significantly improve their writing (Becta 2003).

A context for word and sentence level investigation and exploration

Material can be loaded onto a computer for independent exploration and investigation.

Supporting children with a range of learning needs

ICT can be particularly valuable in supporting lower attaining children so they can access relevant objectives. Support mechanisms to allow access to objectives can include:

- Visual and aural prompts
- Customised word, phrase and sentence banks
- Simplified choice options
- Writing frames and organisational frameworks

Children with very specific needs can also be supported through specially designed ICT applications and hardware. Examples include recorded speech which can be accessed by pupils with limited spoken language. ICT can also provide opportunities for more able children to explore objectives more deeply and broadly. For example, the opportunities offered by the internet for research can provide a challenge for such pupils.

Case studies using word banks and overlay keyboards in independent work

Teachers and assistants can make resources to support children's writing which enable them to work more independently. Children's word-processors such as Textease and Clicker include the feature of a word bank. As noted previously, a word bank allows an adult to input a selection of words and phrases for the pupils, supported by images which prompt recognition. The pupil then has to click on the desired word or phrase to insert it into the word-processing page at the cursor. An overlay keyboard and relevant software can be used in the same way. An overlay keyboard is a rectangular board which is plugged into the computer. It has touch-sensitive pads which can be easily programmed with words, phrases or pictures. Both word banks and overlay keyboards are ideal to support independent writing.

In this first example a pair of children in a year 1 class who would be unable to write independently were able to produce a polished piece of writing. The teacher set up an overlay for a concept keyboard to support them in writing instructions on how to make a sandwich. More complex spellings were provided with the words the teacher thought might be needed – including time connectives, for example, 'first', 'next', 'after that' and 'finally'.

In the second example a reluctant nine-year-old writer was able to complete a piece of writing successfully using a word bank. Shaun had thoroughly enjoyed the visit to the mining museum and asked interesting and informed questions. To ensure his enthusiasm didn't wane, the teaching assistant who supported him prepared a word bank in Textease of words and phrases she thought Shaun would need. He wrote for longer than ever before and finished a piece of work, which was displayed. This increased his confidence and self-esteem and gave him a more positive attitude when writing with pen and paper.

Good use of adult support in guided and independent work

As noted earlier in this chapter, many teaching assistants have considerable experience and skill in delivering guided reading and writing sessions because of their involvement in intervention programmes. These skills could be utilised to extend to ICT texts. The teacher could provide some support in planning appropriate sessions using talking books or non-fiction ICT texts. Suitable NLS Framework objectives would need to be chosen and linked to the appropriate year and term and the needs of a particular group of pupils. The assistant could then follow the recommended structure of guided reading. Similarly, guided writing sessions can be delivered by a teaching assistant using suitable objectives and supporting independent writing with a group of pupils using laptops or desk top machines.

Some adult support during independent work is also likely to enhance pupils' learning. Pupils need someone to turn to with particular technical problems or they may need prompts to focus them on the task in hand. The teacher, however, needs to ensure that adult support is not over-directed and that children are allowed to learn independently or from peers rather than be over-reliant on adults. A goal of the use of ICT in education is that pupils are able to use technology independently and appropriately, but help does need to be on hand and this can be problematic if the teacher is engaged in a guided session. The assistant or adult support should not simply sit with the children while they are at the computer, but should prepare specific resources and activities and be part of the planned provision for the lesson. However, children may not experiment if an adult is telling them what to do and what keys to press. The right balance needs to be created.

Relevant research and inspection evidence: using speech feedback software and talking books

Moseley et al. (1999) noted effective practice in primary English teaching in lessons during which children developed an extended piece of writing using speech feedback. The talking word-processor 'read' a passage and the pupils identified mistakes and aspects they could improve. After two months' work, the pupils' reading ages had improved by an average of almost seven months. The writing tasks also showed improvements in punctuation and structure. The effective use of ICT included developing redrafting skills using speech feedback. Using word-processors with speech facilities can motivate pupils to read more and understand a text more easily. Speech support can help with unfamiliar words by providing spoken definitions to extend vocabulary (Moseley *et al.* 1999). Programs with speech support would be useful additions to independent work in the literacy hour.

Research detailed by Becta (2003) includes the points that pupils who use word-processing in combination with teacher guidance significantly improve their writing, as do pupils who write for a real audience. Teachers could plan some regular sessions of guided writing using ICT as one method of implementing this research finding.

Research also demonstrates that talking book software can complement reading instruction. In a recent study using talking books over a four-week period, there were positive effects on reading development and motivation. The teachers and children were extremely positive about the resource. However, the teachers did note that appropriate features in the software need to be chosen carefully to relate to particular pupils' needs. Software designed for early readers can be helpful in developing sight recognition of key vocabulary. On the other hand, more enhanced software which provided hints to support independent word identification was seen as beneficial for children with higher reading levels (Lewin 2000).

Specific gains have been made by pupils with SEN, especially in speech recognition and word-processing (Cook 2001). However, the focus is still on technology supplementing and extending but not replacing adult support. Access to hardware and opportunity to use it are not enough. Children working with ICT need more experienced helpers to model learning, to help sort out problems and to encourage discussion and reflection upon the learning, to ask appropriately challenging questions and to offer information when needed. Children can use ICT without adult support but adults do need to be able to help out if necessary. ICT is most effective when it is fully integrated into a long-term plan for literacy and language (Moseley *et al.* 1999). In practice, this would mean that when planning a unit of work, guided and independent work involving ICT would be involved from the outset and, over a period of time, a range of access to texts would be planned including ICT texts.

Speaking and listening

When learners collaborate on a task in front of a computer or other ICT resource and negotiate decisions, participation and make compromises, speaking and listening tends to be an intrinsic part of the work. Computers also mean that adults sit alongside pupils rather than face them, and so a more collaborative approach can ensue. The speaking and listening objectives from the primary national strategy (DfES 2003c) do contain some implicit links to ICT use, for example: media presentations are considered in year 1, video extracts in year 2, a broadcast in year 3, carrying out an ICT task effectively in year 4 and contrasting TV programmes in year 5. ICT is seen as a medium for speaking and listening. Opportunities across the curriculum are noted in the guidance materials, including how ICT can be built into speaking and listening.

During guided sessions ICT can mean that texts are clearly presented, so opportunities for discussion are enhanced and material can be presented in the plenary session in electronic format. During independent work children can have more opportunities to share ideas if they are working collaboratively using an ICT text. Displaying the text clearly may enable pupils to take a step back and evaluate their work more independently and critically. The potential for making substantial changes to texts is always more obvious and explicit with ICT texts and this can also encourage a more evaluative and discursive approach.

Inclusion and support for learning

ICT can be used in many ways to give access to literacy activities in literacy teaching and the literacy hour and to support the preparation of differentiated activities. Communicating with symbols is one example of how pupils with learning difficulties can be given access to learning in more independent contexts, such as the literacy hour. Symbols resources are available from Widgit Rebus, Picture Communication System or the Makaton range. Software such as Writing with Symbols 2000 and Clicker facilitate communication particularly with pupils with severe learning difficulties. Other children for whom English is an additional language may use symbols as a support for a limited time (Abbott 2002).

Predictive word-processors may also offer support for some pupils, for example dyslexic pupils or some pupils with physical disabilities. A predictive word-processor tries to guess the word that is being typed and this provides support for pupils for whom writing is a particularly difficult and onerous procedure.

The potential for creating differentiated activities with word banks and overlay keyboards has already been discussed. Writing frames can also support children with particular needs. A ready-made file can be created with sentence beginnings to support writing an account such as 'The first place we visited was...'. A newspaper file can be created with headings and sub-headings or a file with ready-made images inserted for selection copying and pasting. However, it is important to note that sometimes supporting pupils also masks their difficulties. A piece of writing produced with a word bank or writing frame is very difficult to assess as some of

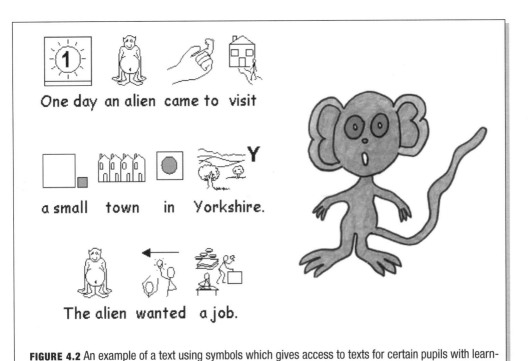

One day an alien came to visit

a small town in Yorkshire.

The alien wanted a job.

FIGURE 4.2 An example of a text using symbols which gives access to texts for certain pupils with learning difficulties. (Used with permission of SymbolWorld – www.symbolworld.org – and Widgit Software – www.widgit.com)

the decision making on word choices and spelling has been carried out by the teacher or assistant who set up the file. This does need to be considered and the support of word banks and writing frames needs to be gradually removed so that progress is made towards writing independently.

Creative uses of ICT

The Books Alive project at Kingston University (Wood *et al.* 2003) surveyed existing talking book provision and use in schools and concluded that talking books were not used for challenging and developing higher order skills. The project directors are in the process of creating materials which will become available on the internet. They are using quality picture books with multi-layered meanings to explore how children can navigate text using information from the interface between visual and printed material. The first resource is based on *Voices in the Park* by Anthony Browne and aims to exploit the full potential of this technology by producing a resource that is genuinely creative and appropriate for pupils at key stage 2 to develop higher order reading skills.

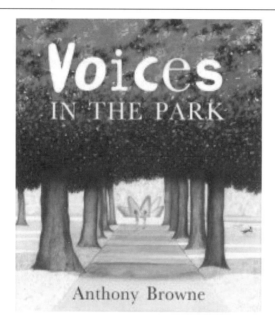

FIGURE 4.3 *Voices in the Park* by Anthony Browne

Future developments

This chapter has outlined ways in which ICT work can be developed during guided and independent work in a literacy session or literacy hour. The improvement in range and quality of electronic texts will support continued development. However, teachers' attitudes may also need to shift for changes in practice to become established. Accessing and interrogating electronic texts and being able to make judgements about the value and reliability of such texts are vital skills in the twenty-first century. Media texts also need to be viewed as significant and worthy of study and as motivating stimuli to writing. Writing effectively and efficiently using word-processors is another fundamental skill. Guided work can provide an excellent way of teaching specific literacy skills involving ICT and can provide a structured and sensible way of making optimum use of hardware such as wireless laptops, and small groups of desktop machines.

Further reading

Access the CD-Rom *ICT in the Literacy Hour: Independent Work and Guided Reading* for further examples of guided and independent work in the literacy hour.

Department for Education and Skills (2003a) *ICT in the Literacy Hour: Independent Work and Guided Reading*. London: DfES (Ref: 0015/2003).

Detailed guidance on guided reading can be found in Bickler, S. (2003) *Book Bands for Guided Reading*, 3rd edition. London. Reading Recovery National Network. This book provides a list of resources at different guided reading levels and examples of plans for guided reading at each level. It is relevant to the Foundation Stage and key stage 1. For examples of guided reading at key stage 2 you will need to access A. Hobsbaum (2003) *Guided Reading: A handbook for Teaching Reading at key stage 2*. London: Institute of Education.

Web links

Widgit (symbols) http://www.widgit.com – this site provides a useful source of symbols and ready prepared files which can be used to support differentiation for a range of pupils with additional needs, including pupils with speech and communication difficulties, writing or reading problems and pupils with English as an Additional Language.

Symbol world is also a free website for symbol users that provides a range of useful resources http://www.symbolworld.org/

The Inclusion site: http://inclusion.ngfl.gov.uk – this site provides a range of information on inclusion. Examples are given of how ICT can support specific disorders and provide support for aspects of literacy development.

The DfES site: http://www.standards.dfes.gov.uk/literacy/publications – you will be able to find relevant DfES publications on speaking and listening and ICT and English in this site.

References

Abbott, C. (2002) *ICT and Literacy Teaching*. Reading: National Centre for Language and Literacy.

Beard, R. (2000) 'Clarion call for another century.' *Times Educational Supplement*. 6 October. Curriculum Special p. 7.

Becta (2003) 'What the research says about using ICT in English.' Web reference: www.becta.org.uk/page_documents/research/wtrs_english.pdf (accessed 8.8.05).

Bickler, S. (2003) *Book Bands for Guided Reading*, 3rd edn. London: Reading Recovery National Network.

Browne, A. (1998) *Voices in the Park*. London: Doubleday.

Cook, D. (2001) 'Meeting the challenges: ICT, early literacy and the role of the educator' *Education*, 3–13 March 2001, pp. 27–32.

DfEE (1998) *The National Literacy Strategy: Framework for Teaching*. London: DfEE.

DfEE (1999) *Training Modules: Writing*. London: DfEE.

DfES (1992) *Curriculum Organisation and Classroom Practice in Primary Schools*. London: DES.

DfES (2003a) *Excellence and Enjoyment*. London: DfES Publications.

DfES (2003b) *ICT in the Literacy Hour: Independent Work and Guided Reading*. London: DfES.

DfES (2003c) *Speaking, Listening, Learning: Working With Children in Key Stages 1 and 2*. London: DfES.

Dewsbury, A. (1999) *Shared and Guided Reading and Writing at Key stage 1*. Oxford: Ginn Heinemann Professional Development.

Goldberg, A., Russell, M. and Cook A. (2003) 'The effect of computers on student writing: a meta-analysis of studies from 1992-2002.' *Journal of Technology, Learning and Assessment*, 2, 1. Available on www.jtla.org. (http://www.bc.edu/research/intasc/jtla/journal/v2n1.shtml accessed on 8.8.05).

Graham, J. and Kelly, A (2000) *Reading Under Control*, 2nd edn. London: David Fulton.

HMI (2000) 'The teaching of writing in primary schools: could do better.' Web reference: www.ofsted.gov.uk/publications/index.cfm?fuseaction= pubs.summary&id=957 (accessed on 8.8.05).

Hobsbaum, A (2003) *Guided Reading: A Handbook for Teaching Reading at Key Stage 2*. London: Institute of Education.

Lewin, C. (2000) 'Exploring the effects of talking book software in UK primary classrooms.' *Journal of Research in Reading*, 23, 2, pp. 149–57.

Makgill, J. (1999) *Guided Reading: Going Solo Under Instruction*. London: United Kingdom Reading Association (UKRA).

Medwell, J., Wray, D., Minns, H., Griffiths, V. and Coates, E. (2002) *Primary English Teaching Theory and Practice*, 2nd edn. Exeter: Learning Matters.

Moseley, D. and Higgins, S. (1999) *Ways Forward with ICT: Effective Pedagogy Using Information and Communications Technology for Literacy and Numeracy in Primary Schools*. Newcastle: University of Newcastle.

Wood, R., Rawlings, A. and Ozturk, A. (2003) 'Towards a new understanding: the "Books Alive!" multimedia project.' *Reading Literacy and Language*, 37, 2, pp. 90–3 (http://www.kingston.ac.uk/booksalive/ accessed 18.09.05).

5

Making full use of your school's ICT resources

Chapter overview

Primary schools, after major targeted funding by the government, have generally become very well-equipped with ICT hardware and software in the past few years. The management of all this equipment is very important, particularly in small or overcrowded schools. Different schools organise their ICT in very different ways – computer suites, scattered computers in corridors or classrooms, shared spaces with interactive whiteboards and an assortment of moveable hardware. The classroom practitioner, teaching literacy in these spaces, may have had very little say in their design and organisation. The equipment available usually reflects a history of enthusiasms and initiatives rather than a coherent and planned set of resources, and this can bring all kinds of problems of compatibility and access.

This chapter will look at the various opportunities for the development of literacy offered by these environments. It will address some of the management issues arising from limited access to computers, and also ways to maximise the quality of learning – particularly in speaking and listening – for which ICT can provide a powerful catalyst. It also includes a detailed examination of interactive whiteboards and their use, as well as practical ideas to make best use of access time in a computer suite.

Different configurations of ICT equipment

    A Computer suites

    B Scattered computers in corridors or classrooms

    C Shared spaces with interactive whiteboards

A Computer suites

It is increasingly common for a primary school to have a computer suite. When computers were first introduced to primary schools, they were generally placed individually in classrooms. When schools were connected to the internet as part of the National Grid for Learning initiative, many primary schools suddenly increased their computer stock and in many cases switched to 'industry standard' Windows PCs. The NGfL agenda was to connect each school to the internet, so primary school networks were set up to allow this to happen. Many schools decided at this point to concentrate all their computer resources into one room – a model they had seen in secondary schools. Falling rolls had often left an empty classroom which could become an ICT room. There were significant economies of scale in wiring one room rather than the whole school, and many teachers were attracted by the idea of a dedicated computer room which would give timetable priority to ICT. There would be the possibility of focused ICT lessons for groups and classes.

In many schools this has worked very well, but over time a few snags have become apparent. A network room needs to be timetabled quite tightly, but the constraints of the primary school curriculum – literacy and numeracy times, assemblies and so on – mean that many suites remain idle for a lot of the time. For some teachers the network room has also meant the loss of an ongoing everyday strand of ICT within their own class area.

Now the educational climate is changing once again. With the current emphasis on embedding ICT into all subject areas, there is perceived to be a need for ICT equipment to be located where the children are actually working. Wireless networking is now available which could allow a network to be dispersed throughout the whole school and even used outside the school walls. This involves installing a card in each computer and a 'hub' somewhere nearby which receives signals from the computers. There is typically some loss of speed, particularly over distance, but this is now a very effective way of avoiding wiring. Sets of wireless laptops on a charging trolley can be taken anywhere in the school and used on the children's own tables – which is probably the best environment for ICT from a pedagogical point of view. Meanwhile, in most schools, the computer suite will probably be with us for some time, and continues to provide a challenging environment for the English teacher. In this section we will consider a few specific challenges and a few strategies to help the class teacher make the best use of these spaces.

A suite consists of a number of computers in one room or area. These may be individual 'stand-alone' computers which work quite independently, or they may be networked together. Networked computers make it easier to install and upgrade software. They allow any pieces of work that the children save to be retrieved and worked on at any computer in the room. They also allow 'real time' shared work of various kinds, such as a collaborative 'newspaper' project where a number of children contribute immediately to the same document, although this is still relatively rare.

Many computer suites have been installed very quickly in response to spending deadlines, and sometimes they are put together with much more emphasis on the technical and economic aspects of ICT than pedagogical ideas. They can have inbuilt problems for English teaching.

- The computer base units and monitors may be so large that they fill all the desk surfaces, leaving no room for paper or books. Most literacy activities will involve the use of paper media alongside the computer.

- The computers may be placed too high or too close together for comfortable collaboration – often a small room is crowded with equipment. Literacy work is often more effective when it involves collaboration and conversation.

- They may be placed so that the children face the wall, making it hard for the teacher to maintain eye contact with the children, and at the same time making it difficult to organise any collaboration or group work.

- The continuous background noise of computer cooling fans – very necessary with fast new processors – and the associated dry atmosphere, may make it an uncomfortable area in which to talk to a class.

- There may be very little space for display, which makes it difficult to give priority to children's writing produced using ICT.

- There are the usual problems of timetabling a shared area. The 'stranded' nature of the timetable with many classes having literacy hour at the same time tends to mean that everybody may also require the computer suite at the same time.

Improving the environment: some hints and questions

Many of these problems can be avoided or reduced with proper planning and design of the computer suite from the outset. Most schools only discover the problems after the room is organised, so here are some practical suggestions to help:

- Try moving computer base units on to the floor to release desk space. This is often a real possibility. It may require holes to be cut in the wall side of benching for wires to be threaded through. If funds allow, switch to wireless keyboards and mice. They are now very cheap – but will require new batteries occasionally. These will reduce the desktop clutter of wires. Be careful that units on the floor are not too near to children's swinging feet, and still provide easy access for CD drives and memory sticks.

- If funds allow, begin to replace large monitors with flat screens. This releases space for children's books and papers to be used alongside the computers, and the new screens are increasingly energy efficient.

- Provide upright plastic document holders and book stands.

- Look at the way the furniture is organised. Is it possible to regroup the whole room (or part of it) in 'islands' which encourage collaboration and communication, rather than having a ring of children facing the wall? This may mean some additional expenditure on wiring and sockets, but it will be money well spent.

- What is displayed in this space? Does the room suggest that ICT is somehow separate from the rest of the curriculum? Is children's work on show? Does it encourage creativity, or is it a sterile, technical zone? What does the computer suite say about teaching or learning priorities?

- Might the screensavers display useful or topical information, even a 'poem of the week', or be another space to display creative work?

- Are there additional tables, stationery, reference books, and so on for non-computer work?

- Are monitors angled for the comfort of the children, or facing up to the teacher?

- Starting lessons in the computer suite can be slow and complicated. If children have to log in to their class 'area' of the network, can this process be simplified? Passwords need to be as short as possible, or a group of children can be responsible for 'logging in' before the lesson begins.

- Are reference materials – dictionary, encyclopaedia and so on – available in the room?

Web links

For further ideas and information see: www.ict.oxon-lea.gov.uk/ICT_docs/teaching_comproom.pdf – teaching in a computer room

http://easyweb.easynet.co.uk/~etfreedman/lessonintro.htm – Terry Freedman's practical guide to getting the most out of a computer room.

With imagination, a computer suite can be used in a variety of ways. Each class can book a slot so that literacy hour can take place here on a regular basis – say, once a week – with each section having a special focus on ICT-linked activities. This takes a great deal of initial planning, but has benefits of focus and motivation, as well as cutting down on disruptive transitions.

Where the timetable allows, the suite can also be used for a group of children working with a teacher, teaching assistant or other adult. There may be times in which the suite is openly accessible to children for routine word-processing tasks.

Creative uses of a computer suite

The computer suite is a great asset to the teacher of literacy, but can sometimes be used in an unimaginative and uninspiring way – if it is ever used at all. We feel it is very important for literacy activities to be engaging, constructive and creative – that is what communication, writing and reading are all about. Here are a few literacy activities which make full and creative use of a computer suite or network room for almost any age group of children.

Newspaper day

A computer room can be transformed into a virtual printing and publishing house for a school newspaper. Most of the processes involved in creating and publishing a 'real' newspaper now take place in a computer environment. After learning about the real-life production of newspapers, children are split into teams as reporters, editors, photographer, picture editor, advertisement organisers, layout designers and so on. Material – interviews, articles, reviews, digital photographs, fact files collected from the internet – is collected over a period of time and stored on the network, then in a 'newspaper day' everything is brought together. This may be made into a dramatic simulation of a real newspaper by emailing copy of breaking stories to the teams, who research, illustrate and compose text to a deadline. Articles may need to be reduced or edited to fit available space. The *TES* has run a newspaper day like this as a national event in March of each year – a very successful and motivating day for children's writing.

Cumulative stories

Good use can be made of a room full of computers by encouraging collaboration. Give each child a one-sentence story starter to type into their computer and ask them to continue the story. After a few minutes (use an egg timer, perhaps) everybody changes computers and picks up someone else's story, a process which can be repeated a number of times throughout the session. This creates a tremendous buzz of reading and writing, and produces a large quantity of text which can be developed or extended in different ways.

On most networks it is possible to save a document and allow someone else to edit or extend it. True simultaneous collaboration is more difficult to organise – usually if one person has a document open, then the software does not allow other people to open it. One impressive exception is the database package 2Investigate (from 2Simple software). If you create a new 'card' in the database, it is instantly visible to all the other users. All the cards can then be sorted, for example into alphabetical order. It would be very useful to have word-processing software like this which could allow documents to be compiled and edited by a group across a network – software developers please note!

Using the program 2Email (from 2Simple software) children can have a 'virtual email' experience which does not use the internet and is therefore completely safe from internet viruses and any occasions for unsuitable content and contact. If this program is installed on a school network it opens up possibilities for all kinds of collaboration. A cumulative story as described above can develop in a series of email exchanges. A story can be forwarded to another child or group, who can edit it, redraft or extend it, then forward it again. Children can write a paragraph about a particular month of the year, animal, place, and so on, and compile these into extended texts. Of course, all these are easy to do with 'real' email if the children have their own email addresses – something which is usually avoided now in favour of open class email addresses.

Building an interactive story together

An interactive web-based island story

Objectives
To create a series of linked web pages which tell a group of stories connected to a clickable map of an island.

ICT objectives
Effective use of Microsoft Publisher as a web-design program
Designing appropriate pages using text, graphics and sound
Creating hypertext through the use of page links
Saving as web pages and linking into a group product

This activity covers similar ground to the year 6 multimedia unit in the QCA Scheme for ICT.

Literacy objectives
Story writing – planning using settings, characters and structure.
Planning and presenting an interactive story using storyboards.

Introduction
Draw a simple outline of an island and scan it into the computer, or use a paint package to make one. It may have various features displayed as symbols or pictures. There are various pre-drawn island maps available, e.g. Black Cat logo projects, and My World Islands. If the picture is inserted into a DTP program (Textease, Microsoft Publisher) labels may be placed in suitable places.

The activity starts with this map of an island (on-screen and on individual sheets) which will be the starting point for individual stories. When these stories are created, we will link them all together to make a web site which other children can read and explore.

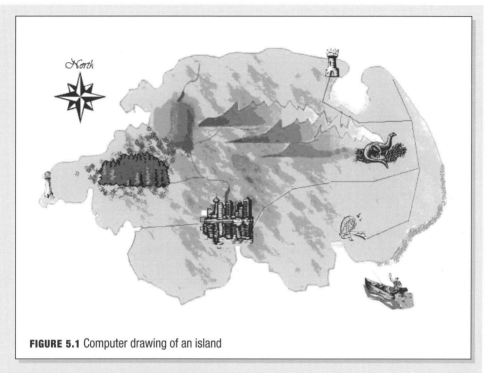

FIGURE 5.1 Computer drawing of an island

Organise children into pairs to plan stories.

1 Setting

Labelling the map. Display the on-screen version of the map on an interactive whiteboard so that it can be labelled with all the children contributing. Each child has a go at inventing names for the different features on the map. They need to think up names which will be interesting and make good settings for stories (5 minutes). Vote quickly on these and establish a common naming for the map.

2 Characters

We want two characters – one boy and one girl. Suggest names and vote. You can tell the story of one or both of these.

If time allows, this part of the story planning can be usefully developed by asking children to draw pictures and/or write descriptions of possible characters.

3 Thinking time

Spend two minutes just staring at the printed copy of the map, letting your mind wander. Then answer these questions with your partner, possibly drawing a line on the map to mark the journey.

- Where are you going to start your journey?
- How are you going to travel?
- Who are you?

- Who is travelling with you?
- Where will your journey end?
- What will you find there?
- What places will you visit on the way?
- What hazards will you meet?

4 Storyboard

Now fill in four 'storyboard' boxes which tell the story in a few sentences. (Try to keep to four, but you can add more later.)

5 On the computer

The following instructions use Microsoft Publisher, as this program converts a series of pages automatically into a website. It is quite possible to use other software – Textease Studio, Microsoft Word – with some adaptation.

Open Microsoft Publisher. Create a 'blank publication' – be sure to select the type: web page. This will not have margins for printing.

Go to Insert and put in three more pages.

Write the story – text is typed into text boxes. Add materials to each page: background colour, word art, autoshapes, clip art, and so on. It's usually a good idea to write the text first before adding other materials. Be sure to make the text quite large, and only use the 'top half' of the page – that's all that will be visible on a web page.

6 Linking the pages

When the stories are written, gather the group together to demonstrate how pages can be linked together. This can be done in various ways.

Text hyperlinks

Any word on a page can become a link to another page. This can bring up a definition of a word, description of a character or place, or can go to 'page 4.' Select the word you want to use, go to *Insert > Hyperlink* and decide which page you want to link to. These links will not be operational until you look at them using *File > Web page preview.*

Picture hyperlinks

Any picture, autoshape or other object you place on the page can become a link to somewhere else. Select the object or picture, right click, choose hyperlink.

Using picture hyperlinks, two trees on a page could become links to two different story pages: a door could lead into a castle; a feature on a map can link to an adventure at that spot – the only limit is imagination.

In exactly the same way, links can be made to internet pages or saved pieces of music or video.

7 Assembling the class story

When each group has finished their story, all the texts can be gathered into one large-scale production. Save each story as a web site (*File > Save as a web page*) giving each one a unique name. Make
sure they are all saved into the same folder. Use a title web page made from the initial Island picture
as a 'clickable map' to call up all the different bits of the story.

   This can be done by using the Publisher 'hot spot' tool (blue circle) to select small sections of the
map and link them to the appropriate story.

   Alternatively, each story can be left as an item in itself – possibly with a contents list which calls up
each one when the reader clicks on a text hyperlink.

   When everything is working properly, the whole story can be copied onto a CD or displayed on a
website.

B Scattered computers

You may have one or two computers in a corner of the classroom, or in the corridor.
Although this has its limitations, in some ways this is quite easy to manage. Almost
any activity in the classroom – particularly written work – can be an occasion for
one or two children to use the computer. It can also be a focus for a small group to
write together in the literacy hour.

Some management tips

■ Keep an ICT log book near the computer. Children can record what they do on
   the computer: date, time, software, any new learning that they think has taken
   place. This will give you a low-maintenance means of monitoring and
   assessing access and computer use.

■ Give named children special responsibility for turning the computer on,
   checking the paper in the printer, keeping the space clear and tidy, and so on.

■ Designate class 'experts' in particular software procedures. This will reduce
   queues and free you for other things. Ideally the computer work should
   proceed as easily as the paperwork!

■ Even if you have no access to an interactive whiteboard, it is possible to gather
   a class around a small screen for a short period of time. Demonstrate new
   procedures and routines briefly with the whole class, then leave a short
   laminated instruction sheet covering the same ground by the computer so that
   children are not asking for help all the time.

■ It's easy to lose track of children working outside the classroom. Hourglasses
   or other timers can help, ensuring a specific activity has a definite time limit.

■ Don't worry too much about equal access or time for all children when you
   only have access to a limited set of computers. While you need to ensure that

children do not monopolise the equipment, it is important to target ICT time to those who need it most. That will mean that children with SEN should have frequent access to the computer for literacy support, and those who are gifted or talented in this area should have opportunities to extend their work. It is vital that children use their time with ICT equipment to add value to their learning, not just to take a turn on at activity which may not be particularly helpful.

C Shared spaces with interactive whiteboards

Two of the most powerful 'drivers' in education today – the trend for more and more effective wholeclass teaching, particularly in the literacy hour, and the trend towards more ICT – have combined to make the interactive whiteboard (IWB) an extremely popular piece of equipment. More and more schools are installing them as a matter of course, and a large amount of government money has been earmarked to pay for them. An interactive whiteboard setup always includes three items: a sensitive display board, a digital projector and a linked computer. The projector displays on the board anything that would normally appear on the computer screen. The screen itself is responsive to touch and is used to control the computer. At present (2005) the market is dominated by two different types of system – 'smart' boards can be controlled by pens which are merely sticks of plastic, or even your finger; 'Promethean' (Activ) boards require a special 'pen' to work.

Whatever 'pen' is used as a controller, it acts in the same way as a desktop computer's mouse, and anything that can be done with a mouse – clicking, double-clicking, dragging – can be done by the interactive whiteboard controller. No special software is required for this, so any program which is already used in school can be used on the IWB. Each board also comes with a range of specific software designed to create lesson materials, but these usually have to be purchased in addition to the board. The most useful feature of these packages is usually a kind of electronic 'flip chart' in which any number of screens can be prepared before the lesson, and which can record and store lesson interactions to be recalled later. There are many other features peculiar to each board – quizzes, hide and reveal facility, clip art, maps and shapes which can be brought onto the screen highlighter pens to annotate texts on the screen, and so on. As the IWB is largely used as a tool to present writing, all these tools have the largest impact on teaching of literacy.

Using the whiteboard the teacher can carry out these typical activities:

- Annotate (circle, highlight) any item which appears on the screen – for example, highlighting language features in a text.
- Create notes during the lesson on a virtual 'flip chart' and save them – modelling note taking.
- Prepare materials which can appear instantaneously on the screen.

- Call up web pages.
- Demonstrate software.
- Display video clips or access television online.
- Convert handwritten text to editable print – this is a feature of some boards.
- Move objects round the screen for sorting, labelling, and so on.
- 'Draw' and 'paint' electronically using large motor movements.
- Involve children in highly visible interactive participation with the lesson.
- Control from the computer with a mouse or graphic tablet as well as the whiteboard pen.

The best place for an interactive whiteboard is in the room or space where you actually teach the class – only then will its use be embedded in the curriculum, rather than just being an aid to ICT teaching. It will require connection to a computer, preferably linked to the school network. This also has cost and wiring implications. The board should be installed:

- At such a height that children can use it effectively, able to reach every part of the screen including the window icons at the top. (2Simple have enterprisingly begun to add a 'pull down' tool to their software, so that short children can 'pull' the screen contents down to a position where they can reach!) Unless the children can participate, the IWB has little value in literacy teaching.
- At such a height that the teacher can use it without continual bending and twisting, which can lead to strain and backache.
- Clear of furniture at the sides so that the user does not cast shadows, especially over what they are attempting to write.
- Preferably mounted on the ceiling – this keeps the expensive and delicate projector bulb out of reach. This is a good idea, as they typically cost £200 or more to replace. If a projector stands on a table there is a constant health and safety risk from wires, and it will also need to be recalibrated every time it is moved – however slightly. Using the 'pen' to write depends on the mark being exactly where you expect it, so calibration is very important.
- In a location where sunlight does not obscure the image, or where curtains or blackout can be applied on particularly bright days.

Children (and teachers) should be given clear guidelines including:

- Don't use marker pens on the board – the board surface is a sophisticated, sensitive and expensive membrane which needs to be treated with respect.
- Don't look into the projector beam. There is a danger of damage to the eyes. As with looking into the sun, children will avoid this effectively, but it should be explained to younger children in particular.

- Take special care of electronic 'pens', remote controls and other equipment – they are expensive to replace.

- Always turn off the projector using the remote control and allow it to cool before switching off at the mains. This will prolong the life of the lamp bulb.

It is advisable to know where a spare pen is kept, or spare batteries for the remote control. The projector can easily be used to display whatever is on the screen of any computer, including laptops, although the board itself will only function if the computer connected to it has the appropriate driver installed. If a laptop is attached to the board, turn it on last of all. Usually it will 'take over' the connection and display correctly. Don't forget that the data projector part of the IWB system is capable of displaying video or DVD quite easily, making it possible for the whole class to view these. This is one reason why these projectors are so popular with school burglars, so also be aware of security issues. Some schools have opted for the much cheaper alternative of installing data projectors without interactive whiteboards. This allows children to see what is on the computer screen and is effective for demonstration, but lacks the motivating and interactive nature of the board.

General management issues

There are several management issues involved in the use of computers in the classroom, particularly in literacy. This section will address some of these potential problems and pitfalls:

Record-keeping

Record-keeping is crucial – children should keep a log of what they have actually done in each computer session, and, more importantly, what they have learnt. A file or book (on paper, or on the computer), which becomes a personal ICT portfolio for each child, could also include dated printouts of drafts and completed work. Literacy-related work will occur across the whole curriculum, and this is an effective way to keep track of it. See the chapter on assessment for more detail on this subject.

Relevance

Keep checking the relevance of the computer activity to what you are trying to teach. Many 'literacy' activities only test children over and over again in a more or less exciting manner. This may not be what you want. If the children understand the work they will find this easy, but if they don't understand it they will merely experience frustration. The computer is not a substitute for a teacher when it comes to explaining and teaching concepts.

Testing

Always try out new literacy software yourself – however briefly – before giving it to the children. This is admittedly time-consuming, but you will know whether it is appropriate, what problems are likely to occur and how to tackle them, when you do not have 30 children to deal with. There are many sources of information about software. It is useful for the teacher to keep up with reviews in the TES Online, Guardian Online, Teem (teachers evaluate multimedia) to get a sense of what good software is available.

Alternative work

Computers sometimes break down – viruses, power cuts, disk failures – and these things always seem to happen when you least expect them. It is advisable to plan a few activities to keep in reserve which do not depend on computers! Remember that if the school network goes down it is still possible to use a stand-alone computer such as a laptop with the data projector or interactive whiteboard.

Opportunities for speaking and listening

However ICT is managed and organised within the school, it can provide many opportunities for speaking and listening. ICT includes tape recorders, sound-sampling, recording to computer, digital cameras and video, and these can enrich this whole curricular area. The discussion of these will lead into a more extended review of the issues involved in speaking and listening, in the light of their prominence in the primary strategy.

In the next section we will explore some ICT implications of the Primary Strategy Speaking and Listening objectives. There are many ways in which ICT can promote and enrich speaking and listening. We shall look at each of the strands in the following three sections:

Listening

Use tapes, videos, CDs and DVDs to develop the skills of concentrated attentive listening and express views. The ICT here offers the ability to repeat and pause the material for focused listening. The children learn 'to select and describe key features of effective media presentations' (10, year 1 term 3). By year 3 their listening media-literacy can be quite developed: now they can identify 'main sections of a video and how these are signalled through voice-over, music and graphics' (30, year 3 term 2). Headphones are very useful for listening work, and a cheap 'headphone splitter' allows two children to listen to a story together without disruption. Learning to use these media is much more powerful if children have access to creating material rather than merely consuming it, for example by using simple digital video.

Media literacy continues to develop as children identify 'key sections of an informative broadcast, noting how the language used signals changes or transitions in focus, for example listening for words and phrases such as 'now', 'then', and 'next' as video moves from presenter to film clip' (34, year 3 term 3; 38, year 4 term 1). The education department of the British Film Institute is a good resource for this work, as is the newly developing BBC Creative Archive.

In year 4, children compare telephone talk with face-to-face communication (45, year 4 term 3) and use television news to compare formal with informal talk, for example 'contrasting excerpts from a national news broadcast and children's TV' (year 5 term 1).

Media texts should also form part of the review process and ongoing conversation and evaluation about films, TV programmes and other electronic texts. 2Review is an invaluable support for this (year 2 term 2; year 3 term 1).

Of course, these moments outlined by the curriculum are only a small part of the continuous listening which takes place in children's lives as they are exposed to mass media of all kinds. Media literacy should underpin every part of the curriculum, so that children learn to discriminate, evaluate and create media products for themselves.

Group discussion and interaction

Many pieces of software, particularly those categorised as 'passive' (in which the user actively creates the content) – for example, My World, LOGO, word-processors – can act as a very good catalyst for group discussion, turn taking and contributing in groups (7, year 1 term 2; 23, year 3 term 3).

Any collaborative writing task involves a great deal of structured speaking and listening, such as taking 'different roles in groups and (using) language appropriate to them, including roles of leader, reporter, scribe, mentor' (39, year 4 term 1). Larger projects such as extended collaborative writing or class newspapers can involve the complex and valuable discourses of planning and reporting back to the class (for example, year 1 term 3; year 4 term 2; year 5 term 1). Although these objectives are given precise locations in each year, their use should of course be much wider. Effective speaking and listening along these lines should be a daily part of all ICT activities. Planning software such as Inspiration or 2Create can support these activities in a powerful way.

The preliminary research for the Impact2 study of ICT in schools showed that children often have a very rich concept of electronic media. This is something which forms a subject of discussion and also stimulates discussion and talk which can extend language.

Drama

Drama can be enriched by recording (audio and video) (8, year 1 term 2; 24, year 2 term 3; year 3 term 2) in which the children can prepare a polished presentation and are able to comment and reflect on other children's work. A word-processor is essential in the creation and duplication of play scripts (for example, arranging scripts on the page, filling out brief notes, expanding on key words as the basis for script writing – 42, year 4 term 2; 51, year 5 term 1). Video extracts may be paused, replayed, tried out with different music (for example, comparing two short video extracts, choosing words to describe effects of costumes, set, lighting and music – to consider how mood and atmosphere are created in a live or recorded performance. 20, year 2 term 2; 61, year 6 term 1).

Future developments

It is very risky to try to predict the future, but it seems inevitable that soon all classrooms will have interactive whiteboards – and very soon replace them with a similar but better product. A teacher commented to me recently that if she lost her IWB she would feel as if she had lost her right arm! Technology becomes smaller, faster, and more powerful. The well-managed classroom of the future may have far less ICT present as large objects – screens, boxes and wires – but far more embedded in the classroom environment, actively supporting teaching and learning.

Web links

Interactive whiteboards:

http://www.btinternet.com/~tony.poulter/IWBs/iwb.htm   – 'Board with Teaching' IWB resources collected by Tony Poulter

http://www.ictadvice.org.uk/index.php?catcode=as-pres_02&rid=4938&section=te – ICT advice on interactive whiteboards

http://www.prometheanworld.com/uk – Promethean ('Activ') boards

www.smartboard.co.uk/ – Smart boards

Video/film resources:
http://www.bfi.org.uk/education/teaching/ – British Film Institute resources

http://creative.bfi.org.uk/ – Creative Archive Licence Group

http://creativearchive.bbc.co.uk/index.html – BBC Creative Archive material

Software
http://www.2simple.com/ – 2Simple Software (2Email, 2Investigate, and so on)

http://www.newsday.co.uk/ – TES Newsday

The effective use of the internet and electronic mail

Chapter overview

This chapter will offer a detailed guide to the use of the internet and email in the classroom. It will describe key strategies needed to find information from the internet quickly and effectively, as well as ways to develop these vital literacy skills with children. The issues of web page validity and internet safety are discussed in detail. Finally we look at the effective use of email in school, and provide a comprehensive directory of web-based resources.

Introduction

Literacy in education is inescapably linked to literacy in society at large – and one of the most conspicuous developments in literacy has been the rise of the internet. For many people, children and adults alike, the first port of call to find a piece of information is no longer a library or even a book, but the internet. As well as this, an increasing proportion of personal communication is text-based and electronically mediated, through email and SMS (text messaging). Paradoxically, this exponential growth of text is seen by many to threaten literacy and book culture. The world of education has responded with various initiatives and projects, attempting to harness new technology and foster literacy.

In 1997 the document 'Connecting the Learning Society', based on the recommendations of the Stevenson Report, reflected a significant change of approach in the use of technologies in our classrooms. The idea that all schools would be connected to the internet represented one of the most exciting and forward-thinking developments in 20 years. It was also a huge and expensive social experiment. The internet is in some ways the best information source in the world, with its usage and content growing exponentially year on year. But the potential of the web is not simply in terms of the amount of information, but of the type and variety that can be accessed, none of which would be available even in the most well-stocked school library. Many of the materials available through this new medium were not written especially for children and many teachers have little experience of using these resources in the classroom. Information literacy is almost a new subject, and teachers need to develop their own competence and confidence before they can help their pupils. There is a need, therefore, for teachers to have support in order to help pupils make effective use of these new opportunities for learning. This chapter will provide some of that support and also look at the ways available today to manage the risks posed by the internet.

Internet literacy 1: how to find information

Effective searching

On a visit to a library, we employ familiar search strategies: we go to the right room, look on the correct shelf, consult the catalogue to find the Dewey reference number. This set of skills quickly becomes second nature to a regular library user. In the far vaster 'library' of the internet, it is equally vital to develop good search strategies to access information. We normally teach children the key skills of paper literacy – using alphabetical order, consulting contents pages, scanning indexes – and yet often approach the internet with much less care and focus. There is already a number of recognisable 'information literacy' skills which apply to all electronic information sources, including the internet, and these must be a necessary part of literacy teaching.

Search engines

The internet is a librarian's nightmare. Anyone with access to the internet can publish or broadcast anything they wish to, without any quality control or editing. Nobody will correct their grammar or spelling, or check the reliability of their facts. Once published, there is no obligation for the author to maintain a site, keep it up to date, or even keep it online. So the world wide web is a constant flux of millions of items of information, almost out of control. Fortunately, among all the chaos there is still a huge amount of useful and valuable information, and the internet is gradually developing structures of labelling and validation.

Search engines are immensely important in this process, making a valiant attempt to mediate or map this chaos for the user – as a kind of automated librarian. They are pieces of software which are created to impose some order on the world of the internet, and they are changing and developing all the time. They use a number of different approaches. In search directories, companies and individuals can register their websites, providing key words and details, rather like getting a listing in Yellow Pages.

More commonly, however, search engines send out software 'agents'. These are automatic travellers which set off on a never-ending journey, following links from page to page, and sending information back to base. This is compiled into a huge catalogue – a database or map of the web which you can visit and search. Since not all web pages have links to other pages, some sites may never be sniffed out by these software agents. Different search engines will certainly find different things.

The most simple search can result in millions of results – and many users will only look at the first ten – so the order in which these results are presented is very important. The ways in which they are organised have become increasingly sophisticated. Google uses a process called 'page ranking'. If a lot of people visit your website and find it useful, they may create links to it. Each link is a virtual 'vote' for your website, and adds value, rather like a bid at an auction. Google places your site higher in the list of search results if a lot of other people give it value in this way. If the site which links to your site is already popular or authoritative, then this 'vote' carries particular weight. Other factors used by search engines include the simple popularity of a site – how much traffic it attracts, and the number of times the word you are searching for appears in the site. All of these are open to abuse by sites which try to falsify their search-engine placing, for example, by repeating key words hundreds of times in their hidden coding. These strategies are sophisticated forms of market research, however objective they seem to be, and the sites they return to your searches may not reflect your own priorities. It is as well to cultivate a critical, sceptical and flexible attitude to all internet information.

You don't normally have to pay to use search engines, as they make their money from advertising. This is usually in the form of a small 'banner' at the top of the screen – or in Google's case, the offering of 'sponsored links' on a separate part of the screen. If, for example, you search for a food-related word, an advert for something edible will appear.

Searching: general guidelines

Many teachers get frustrated and discouraged by the sheer volume of information their searches produce. There are a number of simple ways in which the process of searching can be improved and refined. A good search should return a small number of relevant sites, and this is quite possible to achieve using the following strategies.

Key words

Think carefully about what key words you are going to use before you type them into a search engine. At its simplest level an electronic search uses 'strings' of letters. It is not intelligent – it merely matches letters with other letters. That means that spelling is crucial. If I search for a information about a hippopotamus, 'hippo' or 'popot' will get results, 'hippapotamus' will not. When you are searching, think carefully about the precise words you are looking for. Include synonyms – the document you are looking for might use a similar word to the one you have typed in. An 'early years' search, for instance, might miss documents which only talk about 'foundation stage.'

Singular

Use singular terms as much as possible. Searching for 'lesson' will yield both 'lesson' and 'lessons' – but if you search for 'lessons' the search engine will not return 'lesson' – remember, the computer is matching strings of letters.

Combining words

Think how to combine the key words using logical operators +, –, OR. Putting + immediately before a word means 'include this word in every search result'.

Search for: literacy +KS1 and all the documents you find will contain both words.
Search for: literacy OR KS1 and the documents returned could contain the word literacy or the word KS1. This is a much larger and potentially less useful set of documents.

These operators can also be written in words: if you type 'AND' in capital letters the computer will read it as an instruction – the word 'and' will not be searched for.

Google does this automatically, so in Google there is no need to use + at all. Other search engines sometimes assume that you mean 'OR' if you search for two words – 'Find me *this* or *that*'. Obviously, you will get much better (and fewer) results with AND than OR.

Minus (–) can be very useful. It excludes whole categories of information. 'Lesson plan –K12' will probably exclude many American school resources.

Using quotation marks

When you are searching for an exact phrase or sentence, always surround it with quotation or speech marks. If you search for *Mary Jones* all the Mary's on the internet will arrive with all the Joneses. Putting the phrase in quotes – "Mary Jones" – will only return documents where the two words are together – much better! This will also work with phrases containing common words which are normally ignored by the search engine – "I wandered lonely as a cloud" for example. "Fish and chips" will give sensible results as a phrase – the 'and' is not treated as a search operator when you place it inside speech marks.

These features can all be combined to build up complex searches, for example, several phrases in speech marks added to a number of key words:

"speaking and listening" "national literacy strategy" KS1

A search like this should be quite precisely targeted and yield a relatively small and useful set of results. Adding more key words will make it even more effective.

Special features

Look out for handy 'special features' of search engines. Google allows you to use a tilde (that's one of these squiggles ~ usually found on the keyboard above #) to find near synonyms. A search for *~literacy* will also bring results on *reading* and *writing*. *"Digital camera" ~help* will give you pages which may include *advice, tutorials* and *guides*.

Google has initiated an exciting project to make a library of books completely searchable online. At the moment, even if a book text is on the internet, search engines only return phrases from the first pages of long documents. Amazon is also making many of its books searchable ('search inside').

Intelligence

The intelligence behind a good search lies in the user, not the computer! If you design your search well, you will probably find some good results. But remember that not everything is on the internet! If you search efficiently and come up with nothing, abandon it and go to the library. Some things are exceptionally well-supported on the internet, for example, ICT stuff, personal enthusiasms of collectors and so on. Other areas are hardly represented at all. As with any other kind of literacy, experience will bring a realistic sense of what the internet can and cannot do.

Search engines are a vital tool for finding information, for example, Google, Alltheweb, and Yahoo. You can find out how search engines operate, what new developments are taking place, and comparative listings of search engines at www.searchenginewatch.com.

Instant search

Google has recently offered a new service called Desktop Search – followed in rapid succession by similar services from Yahoo! and Microsoft Search. To use this a small piece of software is downloaded to your own computer, and immediately starts to create a private index of all the documents on your hard drive. This can then be searched in the same way as Google searches the internet. Typing the word 'literacy' into Desktop Search brings up context-snippets of all text documents with 'literacy' mentioned in them, as well as emails and visited websites whose pages still remain on your system. Each document can be opened with a single click of the mouse.

Until the advent of search technology as powerful as this, good practice on the computer entailed having a clear directory structure. An organised user would create folders with clear titles, arranged in a logical and accessible way. This in turn is modelled on the traditional library, with its catalogues and numerical systems to make it easy to classify and find a book. Desktop Search appears to make this hierarchical ordering suddenly irrelevant. Do I really need to organise my information if I can access any item instantly by searching?

Many of us are reluctant to let go of the clear categorising of information in favour of the trivia/soundbite culture engendered by instant search technology, but it clearly has huge implications for education. In some areas this is clearly a very positive development. Information texts – whose structure is already designed for access rather than according to logical development – are obvious candidates for the digital age. In particular, dictionaries, encyclopaedias, telephone directories and catalogues of consumer goods lose very little in translation to an electronic format, and gain enormously in speed and efficiency of access. The multi-volume *Oxford English Dictionary*, for example, is much easier to work with in digital form.

There is, however, a great deal more to textbooks and narrative works than the instant retrieval of unrelated 'facts'. It is also possible to create websites which express, by their links and the arrangement of their pages, a logical or hierarchical flow of knowledge. As teachers, it is increasingly important to use the internet and electronic texts to extend connected thought and logical thinking, rather than being merely a source of instant answers. Barrett's taxonomy of comprehension skills (in which appreciation and evaluation are seen as high level reading skills) applies just as much to electronic materials – and there should always be a gentle pressure on the learner to move towards higher levels of comprehension and interpretation.

Practical examples

At the zoo

In a Becta example, a group of children used a CD-Rom of text and pictures of the animals in San Diego zoo. They were asked to investigate animals' noses and ears. So, instead of finding disconnected facts about zoo animals, they began to ask questions and make connections. Why did certain animals have larger ears? What habitat do they belong to? What would be the advantage to these animals in their particular ecological niche? The best investigations use questions which are fairly 'open' and which encourage an exploring mindset rather than a search for a particular fact or soundbite. This example illustrates the overlap between curriculum areas. Although the children were working in the area of science, they were exercising the literacy of 'reading' a new media text and developing the appropriate language to respond to the information. This particular CD-Rom material and much more is now available on line at http://www.sandiegozoo.org/animalbytes/index.html.

Fox hunting

As a literacy activity, a group of year 6 children had to compile a 'persuasive writing' report about the issue of fox hunting. They were pointed to a number of different websites which presented arguments and statistics on both sides of the issue. They were asked to create a smooth, integrated account which drew on the documents but did not merely print them out or stitch them together.

What lives in the hedge?

Some year 4 children were looking at the hedge which ran alongside their school field, and investigating the wildlife which lived within it or used it as a corridor. They collected information in a database, but wanted to put together a report in the form of a website. They used the program Inspiration to brainstorm ideas and create a concept map or flowchart which would be a design for their website. They drew arrows to indicate connections, attached notes and pictures. Pieces of writing – information texts, stories and poems – were incorporated into the presentation of the hedge. The computer had become a space in which they could clarify and order their thinking, connecting the knowledge they had collected into logical structures – a level of literacy which is increasingly required in our multimedia society.

For reflection

As a society, we have moved from an economy focused on producing material goods to what is called the 'information economy'. In the UK an increasing number of people work with data, information and services that depend on information. The trouble is, there is too much information to take in – we are overwhelmed, drowning in information. Some commentators now see a new emerging stage of social development, in which we are beginning to move from an 'information economy' to an 'attention economy'. (There is a more detailed account of this in Chapter 1.) If you like, the commodity we are short of is no longer information – we have too much of that already – but what we can attend to, what we can take in. The teacher, librarian, knowledge professional, advertiser, tries to make the information engaging to the attention. How can we ensure that children don't just collect soundbites, but that they develop 'attention structures' which can turn data into information, and develop a depth of knowledge and understanding? This is where new literacies are called for. Consider these observations about users of the internet:

- Advice to website designers – if you don't 'catch' the reader in the first ten seconds, they will leave your website.
- Lots of people use search engines, but few people read more than the first ten search returns.
- Although it indexes millions of files, including the full text of books, Google only searches the first 1,000 words of texts.

From these fairly trivial examples, a kind of pattern emerges. It is possible that instant accessibility has its down side: it prioritises the nearest, easiest, most accessible. In using the internet I give most value to what I can reach (hit?) first. The teacher who wishes to develop true literacy, at whatever level, needs to respond to this and find ways to increase attention, enrich structure, and encourage the growth of higher order comprehension. This is no easy task!

Internet literacy 2: collecting and downloading information

This practical section provides guidance on how to collect material from websites on the internet and use it on your own computer. Almost any text or picture which appears on a website can be copied or displayed in a document you are creating – although the normal conditions of copyright apply. It is helpful to understand that a web page is not a single item – like a page of a book – but a collection of different files or objects. A typical web page may include pieces of text and pictures – including logos and navigation arrows or buttons. Each of these can behave independently. You can copy a picture, for example, from a web page, without making a copy of the other items around it. Conversely, if you save a web page, you may find you have a skeleton page with holes where the pictures might be expected to appear. To save the whole web page, you need to save all the items on it.

Saving a web page

On your internet browser (for example, Internet Explorer) click on the file menu (top left) and choose 'save as . . .'. One option is 'save web page complete . . .'. This will save the entire set of files which makes up your web page to an area of your computer or disk. In many cases, this process will allow you to continue to use the web page even when you are not connected to the internet. A saved web page will often have a central file called 'Index'. Double-click on Index to run the website.

There is a more sophisticated approach which will save copies of websites more automatically. Go to 'Favorites' to mark the site you are looking at. Tick the box marked 'make available offline' (see Figure 6.1). You will be prompted to say how many 'layers' you want to save, and then pages will be stored in your computer as you move from one to another, and these will be available when you are no longer online. Be aware that 'active' material – forms and so on – will not work in these saved versions.

Saving text from a web page

When you save the page from the File Menu, instead of 'Web Page (Complete)' choose 'text only' (see Figure 6.2). This will save 'just the text' without any of the colours, fancy fonts or formatting there might be on the page. This is a very

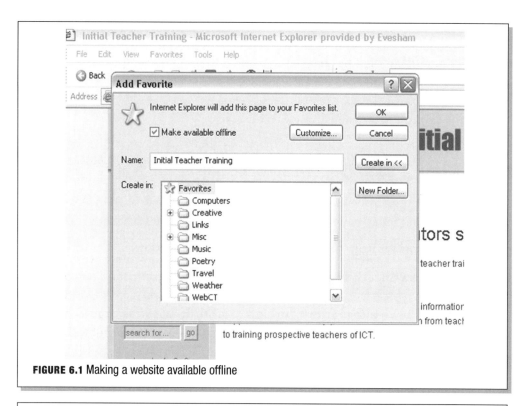

FIGURE 6.1 Making a website available offline

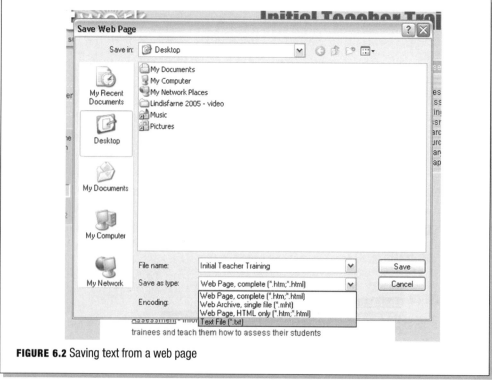

FIGURE 6.2 Saving text from a web page

straightforward way of extracting the text from a site. It creates a very small file which will use very little memory. You can use Word or Wordpad to look at the text file you have created.

Printing from a web page

File menu (or right click) > print

This will print out the page or pages – often annoyingly with one word on the last page! You can choose which pages to print, or, better still, drag your mouse across some text, then 'Print selection' – if you just want to print out a paragraph or column. Alternatively, select some text with the mouse, copy and paste it into a word-processor, where you have more control of the printing process.

Copying and pasting (words, pictures) into a word-processor

It is well worth developing the habit of keeping a word-processor and a web page open at the same time, so you can switch from one to the other and copy material as required. In Windows you can switch by clicking on the document name at the task bar at the bottom of the screen. This is a fundamental literacy skill in handling online information.

Cogitum Co-Citer is a very useful and powerful free tool for creating the collections of texts from the internet. Once it is installed, whenever you select some text

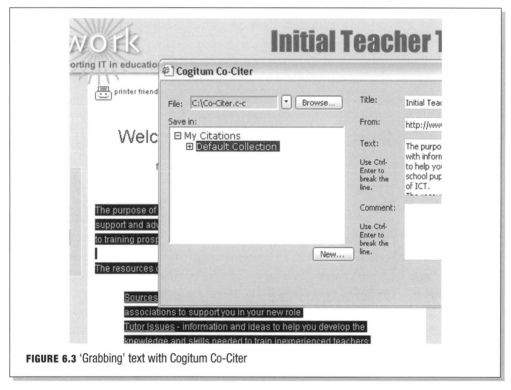

FIGURE 6.3 'Grabbing' text with Cogitum Co-Citer

on a web page, a new option – 'grab selected text' will appear on your right-click menu. This captures the selected text, its internet address, its title and date and adds it to a collection of quotes which can be organised, printed, copied or pasted.

Internet literacy 3: evaluating online information

A teacher is showing a 'big book' to a class of key stage 1 children. She holds the book open where they can see it, pointing out the author, the contents, and possibly the index. She is giving them a simple induction into the protocols of printed text. In adult life we have a vast repertoire of cultural information which enables us to 'judge a book by its cover' – at least to be able to be fairly certain what sort of book we are looking at. Whenever we look at a book or any other printed document, our prior experience of texts gives us a good idea of its validity or authority even before we start to read. In this way a newspaper is easily distinguished from an academic textbook, or a shopping list.

On the internet, all these markers are missing. It is much less easy to assess whether a document is true, reliable or authoritative. Highly convincing and authoritative websites can be created by ten-year-old children with the right soft-ware. 'Phishing' has become a major cause for concern, in which counterfeit versions of bank websites are set up to trap the unwary into revealing their pass-words and account details, and rapidly losing their money.

As the internet becomes established, there are already some conventions which need to be learnt if we are to navigate the internet successfully and safety. These are emerging into a new 'literacy' of information. It is vital for teachers to understand them and communicate them to children as part of their literacy teaching.

The first prerequisite is a general attitude of questioning. People who are very sceptical about information on a printed page can suddenly become gullible and easily fooled when they are presented with web-based information. There are some obvious questions which go a long way towards establishing the authenticity of a web page.

Web page authenticity

1 Who is the author?

Most people would usually pay little attention to an anonymous paper document, but happily use web pages with little or no idea of their authorship. This is an important habit of thought to encourage – to ask the question 'Who is giving me this information?' If a page is 'unsigned', or does not form part of a well-known and reputable public site, you can safely disregard the information contained in it.

There is an important exception to this principle. Sometimes an anonymous page is 'nested' inside a site, and does not carry the 'cover' details. It's just a 'page' in a 'book' and you need to find the 'title page' and 'contents'. This can often be achieved by 'truncating' the web address – namely, take words off it and move up through the site until you find out where it is and who has written it. For instance, on my own website, if you look at this page:

> http://business.virgin.net/sound.houses/ks3/sherlock.htm

you will find a review of the 'text disclosure' program, Sherlock. That document is inside a folder containing presentation slides about key stage 3 literacy, whose address is:

> http://business.virgin.net/sound.houses/ks3/

That in turn is inside my main website folder:

> http://business.virgin.net/sound.houses/

Only on the higher pages will you find my name and details. You can gain a lot of information by 'chopping back' web addresses to the next 'forward slash'. The 'forward slash' familiar from so many web addresses is actually an instruction to the web browser to 'open the next folder, and look for the top document'. A little knowledge of these protocols and structures – the 'grammar' of web addresses – is very helpful in remaining in control as a user of the internet.

2 Find out about the author

Having established the author's name, it is possible to type this into a search engine and find out who they are, where they come from, and what else they may have written. All this information helps you to assess their reliability as a source of information. Don't forget to use quotation marks around the words if you want to look for a particular person, for example, 'Michael Morpurgo'.

3 Where in the world is this page?

The addresses of many websites include a 'country code', for example, '.uk' for United Kingdom, '.au' for Australia, and so on. You won't find '.us' as America is the birthplace of the internet and makes the assumption that all websites are based in the USA unless otherwise indicated. The web address may also tell you what sort of site you are reading. Look out for '.ac' and '.edu' for academic or university sites, and '.gov' for official government pages. It is so easy to move from country to country on the internet that you can easily lose track of where in the 'real world' it is you are looking at.

The internet constantly stores information about itself which may be collected by various pieces of statistics software. See www.statcounter.com for a free web tool which can identify the pathway a visitor takes through your own website, what key words they used to get there, how much time they spent in their visit, and so on. It is important to emphasise to children that all activity on the internet is potentially visible and may be tracked.

4 Find linked sites

If a page contains useful and reputable information, and becomes listed on search engines, it will receive a large number of visitors. Those who use it most, or value it will put links to it on their own sites. In effect, these people are giving it a 'vote of confidence'. It is possible to find this information about any site. You will need to go to the search engine called Altavista and use the 'link' command. This will tell you all the pages which have links 'pointing at' a particular web address. This is what you do. Type the word 'link' followed by a colon into the search box, then type a web address, for example:

link:http://business.virgin.net/sound.houses/

When you click 'search,' Altavista (www.altavista.com) will return a list of linked pages. A link to a site has some similarity to a positive review or recommendation in the world of books. As described above, this information is used by Google as part of their 'ranking' of websites. Those sites with many votes, links from other sites, go to the top of the list returned when you search for a particular subject. They are usually the most reliable and accessible.

5 Non-internet information

It is always a good idea to check information you find on the internet with 'real life' sources such as books. There is a great deal of distortion, propaganda, and misinformation on the internet, and it is important to check and cross-reference material you find. Unreferenced factual information may be out of date, partially quoted, or deliberately placed to mislead people. Texts on the internet may be published without reference to copyright, and, since they are often unedited, may contain a large number of errors. If you want to pursue these issues further, take a look at an excellent article by Alan November, called 'Teaching Zack to think.'

Internet literacy 4: children and the internet

Safety ssues and 'safe' searching

'Sex' is still, apparently, the most frequent search term in the world. It is important to realise that possibly the most common use of search engines world wide is to find sexually explicit material, and it is all too easy for a child to gain access to pornography. Unfortunately, the pornography 'industry' has been a major driver in the technical development of international links and high-speed networks. It is very important, therefore, to make sure that children are protected, particularly in school, and that your professional role as a teacher is also protected. As with every other situation where children are in situations of potential danger – crossing a road, walking near water, and so on – the most effective safeguard is to develop responsibility and care. This should be a major theme, taught and modelled by the teacher, and is unfortunately an essential component of literacy teaching. As practical safeguards I would recommend some or all of the strategies outlined below.

Passwords

Make sure full internet access is password protected, and that this password is not known to pupils. A password that everybody knows is no use at all – it just wastes time as staff or pupils have to type it in. It is advisable to be serious about passwords. A hacker in an action film who guesses a password to access a secret network is fiction. In real life someone looks over your shoulder as you type, or reconstructs the sequence of letters from watching your finger positions. Children get very good at observing teachers! The best filtering and control systems are no use if the children get access to teachers' passwords.

Passwords should be hard to guess. 'Password' 'secret' or 'changeme' are not a good idea. The best passwords are quite short, but include numbers as well as words. A number interleaved with a memorable word would be hard to guess, for example, a pet's name (Fido) blended with a memorable date (1986) could give a password such as f1i9d8o6...

If children use passwords just to log in to their class space on a network (not on the internet), these need to be as short as possible, otherwise the start of their actual writing and thinking will be delayed. Passwords may actually be unnecessary in some school contexts, and if possible should be turned off.

Visibility

Place your internet computers where the screens are visible to others. Even if you can't actually see what is on the children's screens all the time, the fact that you *are* able to see it is a powerful deterrent.

Filtering

Use filtering software to control access to the internet. Cyberpatrol, one of many such packages, has a constantly updated list of blocked sites. Make sure your filtering software controls or blocks access to news groups, where large quantities of pornographic materials are often freely circulated. Bear in mind, however, that filtering software may sometimes allow undesirable lists of site names to appear on the screen, even if it prevents access to those sites. It can also be the case that sites you would use may be blocked unnecessarily – you are not in charge of the list or the values it promotes. Some American schools, for example, control access to sites about evolution.

'Walled gardens'

Use a 'walled garden' service which only allows pupil access to a restricted range of 'safe' sites. However, these may have disadvantages. Innocuous sites may be blocked for no apparent reason, while some inappropriate sites may slip through the filter. Many local education authorities have set up safe local networks for schools, or it is possible to buy into commercially available subscription services such as Espresso. These provide a huge range of learning and teaching resources within an 'enclosed' area of the internet – although some teachers may feel that they remove the surprises and unexpected learning opportunities of the wider internet.

Acceptable use policy

Make sure your school has an 'acceptable use' policy for the internet, and that it is put into practice at every level. This may involve children and parents entering into a contract of internet behaviour. A good example may be found on the Ambleside Primary School site at http://www.ambleside.schoolzone.co.uk/ambleweb/ourrules.htm.

Care with searches

Don't allow unsupervised searching. Always try out a search yourself before doing it with the children. A lot of the thinking about a search – choosing key words, combining them in the best way, using logical operators can usefully be carried out as a class discussion away from the computer. This not only models information literacy, but means the actual search online is fast, effective and focused. Picture searches, such as the Google image search, are useful to gather pictures and illustrations on any topic. They are also so difficult to control that many schools and LEAs have blocked them completely for children's use.

If you want children to use pictures from the internet, the safest strategy is probably to compile your own resource bank of pictures from websites which the children can access in a folder on the network. Also be aware that images are copyright, unless otherwise indicated, in the same way as pieces of music. One recent development is 'creative commons', which allows certain images to be used freely in non-profit-making or educational contexts, and this will probably grow dramatically in the near future.

Turn off the screen

If an inappropriate picture appears on the screen while you are demonstrating, press the monitor button and turn it off, or, on an interactive whiteboard, use the 'blank' button on your remote control. This will not harm the computer, but will maintain your responsibility and protect the children.

Teach awareness

Impress upon children that all activity online is potentially visible to others. Email can be traced, downloaded pictures remain in memory, visited sites are listed somewhere on the computer.

In all of this, remember that the essential context for all these is the children's own, internalised, responsible behaviour. The most secure systems can sometimes break down. In one school children looked over a teacher's shoulder as she logged onto the internet and memorised the password. So even though there was a secure, 'walled garden' system implemented in the school, pupils were able to bypass it and access whatever they wanted. Open, visible, responsible use within a busy, purposeful classroom is the best scenario – and one in which the children will find the internet to be an invaluable aid to their learning.

Web-based literacy resources

Book texts online

There have been several initiatives to place the text of books on the internet. The first and largest of these was the Gutenberg project – placing books online in a standard, plain-text format. Currently Google is working with publishers and libraries to make digital versions of books available on the internet. The main obstacle, obviously, is copyright. Publishers are understandably reluctant to 'give away' texts that they normally sell. So most full-text works on the internet are quite old – out-of-copyright works. In this respect the smallest local library supplies a great deal of material which you will not find on the internet!

However, the 'classic' texts and extracts online have a lot to offer the literacy teacher. It is easy to download the plays of Shakespeare, well-known children's texts such as *Alice's Adventures in Wonderland,* and vast quantities of poetry – mostly pre-twentieth century. This makes it very easy to set up a whole range of activities.

- Create a short playscript from one scene of a Shakespeare play.
- Display a poem or section of story text on the data projector to discuss language features.
- Create missing-word activities or cloze procedures with pieces of classic text.
- Present children with a text extract to adapt into a play on-screen.
- Use desktop publishing to present and illustrate a text.
- Use the computer to highlight language features – children could change all the adjectives to red text, or underline archaic features of a text.

Web links

Here is a selection of sites where you can find electronic texts:

http://www.bartleby.com – Bartleby – a huge range of literature and searchable texts, particularly good for older poetry and fiction

http://www.bibliomania.com – Bibliomania – searchable works of classic fiction, popular fiction, short stories, drama, poetry, dictionaries, research and religious texts

http://etext.lib.virginia.edu – Electronic Text Centre – texts in copyright are only accessible in-house, but there is another huge collection of books which can be downloaded

http://eserver.org – English Server Accessible Online Publishing

http://www.ipl.org/reading/books – IPL Online Texts Collections – internet public library

http://promo.net/pg – Project Gutenberg – the original online archive of electronic texts

http://digital.library.upenn.edu/books – OnLine Books Page – index of online books and other works

Children's literature

Although the texts of the latest Michael Morpurgo or Jacqueline Wilson books are not on the internet, there are many sites with pictures of their covers, reviews, author interviews, and even extracts to give a flavour of the book. Here is a selection of the best:

Publishers' sites

These sites are designed to add value to the books produced by the publishers and can provide a wide range of relevant resources.

http://www.andersenpress.co.uk/ – Anderson Press: authors featured include Melvin Burgess, Anne Fine, Michael Foreman, David McKee, Colin McNaughton, Chris Riddell and Tony Ross

http://www.barringtonstoke.co.uk/ – Barrington Stoke: publishers of books for reluctant, dyslexic and under-confident young readers

http://www.puffin.co.uk/ – Puffin: contains a good authors' biography section

http://www.scholastic.com/ – Scholastic: general educational and literacy material

General children's book sites

http://www.channel4.com/learning/microsites/B/bookbox/home.htm – Book Box http://www.booktrusted.com/ – Booktrust

http://www.strath.ac.uk/Departments/JHLibrary/chint.html – children's
literature internet sites

Links to lots of children's author sites

http://www.acs.ucalgary.ca~dkbrown/authors.html – children's literature web
guide: authors and illustrators on the web

http://kotn.ntu.ac.uk – Kids on the Net: write stories, poems and book reviews as
well as reading those written by children; advice on writing, including tips by
Jacqueline Wilson

http://www.mrsmad.com – Mrs Mad's Book-a-Rama: children's books reviewed
and rated for young readers, parents, teachers and librarians, with games, stories
and jokes

http://www.rif.org.uk – Reading is Fundamental: reading ideas with authors,
poets and illustrators

http://www.readingmatters.co.uk – Reading Matters: children's book reviews

http://www.storiesfromtheweb.org – Stories from the web: Stories, email authors,
write reviews and stories

http://www.ukchildrensbooks.co.uk – UK children's books: A–Z listing of
authors, linked to their own websites

Email

This section will explore the use of email as a way of communicating and sharing
ideas and projects and so enhancing the sense of audience and purpose within the
classroom.

The UK National Grid for Learning was a project to connect all schools to the
internet, and email was to have a major part in this. There were government
pledges that every child should have their own personal email address which
would follow them throughout their school career. Concerns about children's
online safety have modified this target, but email plays an increasingly important
role in education.

Electronic mail occupies an intriguing middle ground between other forms of
communication. A phone call exists in real time: both parties to the conversation
respond immediately to the other. This is described as 'synchronous' communication.
Letter writing is 'asynchronous' – the recipient may not be able to respond for some
days or even longer. This has led historically to the importance of reflective and
considered letter writing, and the teaching of all the related letter-writing skills. Email

has the immediacy of a telephone message, but can still work in the same asynchronous manner as a letter. So a message can be composed carefully and reflectively, but elicit an immediate response. From the point of view of the teacher of literacy, the immediacy of feedback from email can motivate children to write – but may lead them to use rapid, abbreviated and ungrammatical forms of writing. Email can also lead to ill-considered and regrettable responses which cause damage to social networks in many organisations. Newer media such as texting and instant messaging also bring with them new implications for the literacy of communications.

The asynchronous nature of email is very useful in a school context. It means that real written communication can take place – from child to child, class to class, school to school, or to outside agencies – within the time frames of the school timetable. Convenient times can be set for writing email, and for receiving and responding to messages.

Email and texting have become highly significant modes of social communication for young people. Far from ICT signalling the end of text-based culture, there is more text than ever. In this context, it is vital that our taught literacy should address the *quality* of that text in conveying information – as this is an area in which all the traditional skills of communicating effectively through written language are still important.

Quite early in the development of email, it became clear that there was a lack of nuance in email texts which could lead to dangerous misunderstanding. A joking comment in a telephone call looks much more offensive when written, printed and circulated. An emphatic comment can easily appear to be abusive. This led to the use of 'emoticons' such as 'smiley faces' to indicate the mood of the writer, as well as a host of abbreviations such as IMO (in my opinion) which have now developed into the abbreviated language of texting. In school there is no reason why email texts should not be as carefully written as any other, and it is part of literacy teaching to emphasise this. Email may be spell-checked. Material may be pasted in from other word-processed documents, and can be as nuanced or sophisticated as the writer wishes. The key issues are purpose and audience – as with any other written communication. It is worth stressing the 'public' nature of email. Any message journeys across many computer 'nodes' as it moves through the world wide web. At any of these it is possible – though unlikely – for someone to intercept this message. Even if it is deleted, copies may still be recoverable, as various public figures have found to their cost. Confidential information should still only be entrusted to secure systems of communication.

Email safety

There has been great public concern at the danger of email for children, so before looking at practical applications of email in the classroom we will address some of these potential problems.

Anonymity

Anyone can set up an email account (with Hotmail, Yahoo Mail, Gmail or many other services) with any available name. There is no check on the identity of the address holder. Unscrupulous users – such as those who create 'spam' (unsolicited email) – go to great lengths to present themselves as reputable organisations, so that email they send appears to come from banks, or even colleagues and family members. There are real problems then, in that children may not know who they are talking to in their email communications – an opportunity which has been used by paedophiles.

This, of course, is not unique to email. Anonymous and misleading letters have been around for a long time, as well as people impersonating authority figures such as the police. But it is obviously important, for the sake of the children's safety and the integrity of practitioners, to make the school use of email as safe as possible.

Here are some guidelines:

- Don't give out personal information to strangers in email or chat rooms. This includes information about objects of value in your house!
- People may not be who they claim to be – don't believe all you read on a computer screen.
- Bad messages should be reported to a responsible adult straightaway. Don't respond to them.
- Remember that what you are doing in writing an email is public – careful what you say!
- Open discussion is a great safeguard – in families or schools – so that children can be fully informed and develop responsibility.

Again, what is at issue here is the critical literacy of information handling in new media.

Using email in a literacy context

Children develop their speaking and listening skills much more rapidly than they learn to write – possibly because speaking and listening is constantly exercised in the flow of conversation which surrounds a child at home and school. Writing, on the other hand, only rarely finds a meaningful audience. Much of a child's writing in school is only read by the teacher, and only occasionally is there a sense of dialogue in written work which extends and develops writing. This is where email can have a major part to play. It is a written form which can evoke an almost immediate response, and is therefore much more motivating than many other forms of writing.

Extended writing lends itself to email projects. Children send a paragraph of a story to their epals, then reply with another section. Any collaborative writing task gains an added excitement if it is carried out by email. Some accounts of inter-school email projects are detailed below.

Case study: collaborative writing across the Atlantic (from *ICT Advice*)

A year 3/4 class teacher made contact via email with two schools in California, USA. This was thrilling for both sets of children and, after much communication, they finished up with an 'across the Atlantic' piece of creative writing. The British pupils wrote the first paragraph, the Americans wrote the next and so on. The British school then sent the story off to a couple of other schools and it continued to develop.

Benefits include:

A real audience for writing

At its simplest this can be other members of the class, or children in different parts of the school, but can be much wider. Email can be exchanged with partner schools in different areas – urban schools twinned with rural schools, for example. Links can be made with schools in other parts of the world, exchanging information on culture, climate and so on. 'Experts' can be contacted for information – some children's authors maintain mailing lists or are prepared to answer questions. In all of these cases, the children will be highly motivated to write well.

Time to draft and reshape a message before sending it

Email can be prepared offline – either within the email software or in a word-processor. Text may easily be copied from the word-processor and pasted into an email. This means that a response can be considered and traditional letter-writing skills come into play. Although email is used in a casual way, there is no reason why school email should not encourage good use of language.

The possibility of immediate feedback

This single factor makes email highly motivating. Children also need to be made aware of the dangers of misunderstanding or over-strong reaction which can make email so damaging in certain circumstances.

Setting up an email project

Many electronic communication projects fail because when they are set up they focus too much on the medium of communication rather than the content. Participants need to plan very clearly what information they are hoping to exchange. A good starting point can be groups of children who are studying the same topic. Reasons for the project may include:

- The need to communicate without delay

- The opportunity to share draft versions of work
- The opportunity to exchange materials in different formats such as pictures, text, sound and multimedia

Case study: pictures and descriptions

A primary class in Cheshire established an email link with a school in another part of the country. Each class painted a set of pictures of different characters. They then wrote verbal descriptions of each character's appearance. These descriptions were emailed to the partner class, where the children attempted to paint the faces from the descriptions. The highlight of the project was when both sets of pictures were scanned and displayed on the school website. The class teacher commented that he had never seen such engagement and motivation with writing, particularly from boys.

In common with other group activities, email can encourage discussion and the sharing of ideas. It is essential to ensure that pupils have the necessary discussion skills.

Email projects can open up possibilities that would be difficult to achieve by other means – for example, collecting weather information at different places around the world at the same time.

Email projects can be *closed* – email is only permitted within the school. External messages only come in through the teacher. In an *open* project pupils have full email access, but there is much less control or support from the teacher.

According to *ICT Advice*, these following characteristics make for a successful international email project:

- Teachers have clear expectations. It is important to discuss in depth when the project will start and finish, what its aims and outcomes are, which language will be used, and matters such as delays between receiving and responding to emails.
- Projects are supported from the start by management, teaching and technical staff, pupils and parents.
- Projects are coordinated by one person.
- There is a close match of abilities within partner groups. In language projects in particular, learners' ages and proficiency should be matched carefully.
- Participants recognise cultural differences between countries, from different holiday dates, school working days and times of access to email, to approaches to innovation and working outside the school day.
- Project partners are found by using the internet.

Case study: comparing prices (taken from *ICT Advice*)

This project was initiated through a teachers' chat room called Teacher's House, where a primary school teacher in the USA made contact with a teacher in the UK. The project began with year 5 children in the UK contacting children in the USA and requesting information about their hobbies and their Christmas holidays.

The project progressed as the children from the UK investigated the American school's website. Here they found out about the sorts of things their peers liked to buy. The US school checked out similar information from schools around the world, and the children began to compare prices. They then converted all the prices into dollars. The UK school children collected prices of similar objects in the UK and emailed the findings across the Atlantic.

They also sent an email questionnaire to the American children asking about their favourite foods, pets, pop groups and so on, and presented this information in a data-handling exercise.

Case study: comparing localities

Year 7 pupils in a Bristol school worked with pupils in Brisbane, Australia. All pupils were allocated an epal in the partner school and these relationships were to be developed over the pupils' five years at the school. The pupils created a word-processed account of their local area and included a labelled digital image. The reports were produced over several lessons using one of the school's computer rooms. As a homework task, pupils took a digital or traditional photograph or print of their local area that they downloaded or scanned into the computer and later adjusted. A further lesson was spent annotating the image to show the main geographical features. These were emailed to their epals, who reciprocated with a similar report on their local area. They then compared the two contrasting areas in different parts of the world, producing a classroom display. Teachers in both schools closely monitored the content of the emails, in line with the schools' internet policies.

Ground rules

Before starting an email project, it is advisable to establish some ground rules, negotiating these with the children. Matters to be discussed might include:

- What language is appropriate in emails? Email is not a private medium and can be used for both 'one-to-one' and 'one-to-many' messages.

- Names or pen names must always be used, and email should be addressed to a specific recipient, either an individual or a whole class.

- When can email be written, sent or received? Some schools may expect email to be written offline. Email may be checked at random or at set times.

- Should email (and any attachments) be printed out or stored electronically?

Further details on all these issues are available on the ICT Advice site: http://www.ictadvice.org.uk.

ePALS

If you want to set up an international email literacy project, ePALS is one of several organisations committed to the use of email to enrich the curriculum. It describes itself in these terms:

> The world's largest online classroom community and leading provider of student safe email. Over 4.6 million students and teachers are building skills and enhancing learning with ePALS. Established in 1996, ePALS has 103,034 classroom profiles bringing people in 191 countries together as cross-cultural learning partners and friends.

Discussing books by email

In many parts of the world, the discussion of books characteristic of reading groups and literature circles has become an online activity. A book is chosen by a group of schools and within a set period of time intense email discussions about the book take place between pupils in the different schools. The fact that all the responses are written makes this a particularly powerful context for literacy learning.

Future developments

The internet is in a state of constant change. New technologies appear every day, and many of them are likely to have serious implications for the literacy teacher in the future. The rate of technological change is such that the mobile phones in children's pockets may soon be more powerful computing devices than the classroom computer. Various research projects are looking at the possibilities of harnessing this power for education. The technology which is developing mobile phones could eventually offer calculator-sized devices which could create text, record speech, take pictures and send this material to the school network for composing and printing. It also offers opportunities for collaboration and video-conferencing over distances. Linked with e-learning packages, mobile devices could give personalised support to learners with special needs, translation to pupils learning English as an additional language, and so on. In the future these devices will probably incorporate GPS (global positioning systems) and digital video as a matter of course, opening up many exciting and creative opportunities for literacy education.

Web links

http://www.literacymatters.org/adlit/questioning/after.htm – a good introduction to online literature circles

http://teacher.scholastic.com/professional/techexpert/litcircles3.htm – an overview of using online literature circles

http://learnweb.harvard.edu/2821/r2000_4.cfm – an overview of book clubs online and a sample classroom scenario

http://www.cogitum.com – Cogitum Co-Citer

http://www.anovember.com – 'Teaching Zack to think'

http://www.cyberpatrol.com – internet safety software

http://creativecommons.org – Creative Commons

http://www.ngfl.gov.uk – National Grid for Learning

http://www.epals.com/community – epals online classroom community

References

DfEE (1997) *Connecting the Learning Society – Consultation on the National Grid for Learning.* London: DfEE.

Unsworth, L., Thomas, A., Simpson, A. and Asha, J. (2005) *Children's Literature and Computer Based Teaching.* Maidenhead: Open University Press.

Planning and assessment in ICT

Chapter overview

This chapter offers a set of thoroughly worked-out resources to help with the integration of ICT into literacy planning. Software, hardware and web materials are cross-referenced with other sections of the book. Assessment is explored, particularly the common ground between ICT and literacy, ways of assessing process and keeping records effectively, and a review of assessment resources available to the primary teacher.

Planning

In the planning section below, there is a comprehensive list of activities designed to provide support for planning broadly based on the NLS objectives for each half term throughout the primary school. If you want a full table of these tasks matched and referenced to individual NLS objectives, visit Andrew Rudd's website (http://www.freespace.virgin.net/sound.houses/).

There are three different 'layers' of suggested activities.

A Interactive whiteboard (IWB) activities

These boards are appearing in many schools, and are rapidly becoming an indispensable part of classroom equipment and culture. In a few years, they, or their equivalent in newer technology, will become as unexceptional as notebooks, pencils and blackboards. Meanwhile, there is a need to plan specific activities to utilise this expensive equipment effectively. Some of the activities described are generic – you can use them in many different contexts. Others are specific to particular objectives and software packages.

There are several 'generic' ways in which the interactive whiteboard can be used to support teaching and learning – ways in which it can be used daily as part of literacy work. These are largely taken for granted in the planning suggestions that follow.

1   The use of interactive whiteboard/data projector to display a text for class reading or discussion

2   The use of IWB to demonstrate a new piece of learning (teacher use)

3   The use of IWB to display a text to highlight language features (teacher/pupil use)

4   Use of IWB for interactive work with text – restructuring, redrafting, replacing words, reordering lines or sentences (teacher/pupil use)

B Essential ICT use

These are examples of software or hardware which facilitate a particular learning objective in a way which would be difficult to achieve without the use of ICT. The ICT in these examples provides a better, easier or quicker way to learn. The ICT is not an afterthought, but is fully embedded in the curriculum.

C Extension ICT use

These are examples of software or hardware which enrich and add value to a particular objective. These may extend children's learning and may also link into other areas of the curriculum. Although possibly not essential or mandatory, these activities can motivate children, and sometimes raise them to a much higher level of achievement than would otherwise be the case.

'Generic' word-processing and desktop publishing activities

Here are some ways in which word-processors may be used almost every day. Once they are fully established, these will be largely taken for granted in planning.

1   'Always on' use of a word-processor for routine tasks: a computer in the classroom, a wireless laptop or Dreamwriter, or free access to a corridor cluster of computers or other network space.

2   'Always on' use of a word-processor for SEN support, namely whenever children need the supported writing environment of a word-processor, they can go and use it as an alternative to paper.

3   'Always on' use of a word-processor for the extension and support of gifted and talented pupils, namely whenever children need the extended writing environment of a word-processor, they can go and use it as an alternative to paper.

4   Use of a word-processor for everyday collaborative writing tasks or publishing by a small group.

5   Publishing 'job' – use a DTP program to make a poster or similar publication for any area of the curriculum.

6   Publishing 'job' – use a DTP program to present a story for publication, create a book.

All levels (KS1 and 2) – using the IWB to display text

In reception and year 1, use the interactive whiteboard in any session where it is necessary to display rhymes, texts, and word lists. Children can draw rings around or highlight particular sounds, letters, clusters, words. In this way the IWB can contribute greatly to whole class exploration of words. As children's understanding of spelling develops in years 1 to 3, any texts which are used with the children can be displayed immediately to show, highlight and model spelling features.

To support sentence-level work, display any text which is being used for discussion. Model various text processes – editing, deleting, substitution and replacement of nouns with pronouns, adjectives with stronger adjectives, and so on. Children find this a tremendous help to understanding.

Try to ensure that children take control of the pointer as much as possible, and do the actual selection of words themselves, rather than have the teacher demonstrating everything. This makes for a high level of motivation, as well as engaging the different intelligences of children.

In text-level work, all kinds of written text can be displayed on the IWB for shared and guided reading. Delete words or phrases to leave spaces in the text. Children can develop their cueing skills together as they predict the missing words. Use the IWB wherever possible to model the actual process of writing – elaborating and transforming text – as well as combining pictures and text using programs such as 2Publish, 2Create and Clicker.

If you present poems on the board, it is easy to hide or reveal lines to aid memorisation. Displayed poem texts can be used to discuss and highlight language features – for example, picking out rhymes in different colours. To explore playscripts, display and discuss brief examples, and add these to a class bank of texts. It is very effective to model shared/guided writing interactively, and also to display children's own texts occasionally for group proof-reading and a sensitive discussion of language features.

IWB activities suitable for different levels

1 Whole class phonics (word level work) reception, years 1–3

The website of Camelsdale First School has an inspirational collection of whole class PowerPoint slide shows which are free to download. These address common issues such as simple phonics, high frequency words and many other literacy topics. They are inspirational in that they provide simple templates to create your own activities. The material a teacher uses to explain a new idea to the whole class can immediately become a reinforcement activity as a child models the teacher's role in a small group.

2 Word lists (word level work) reception, year 1

It is a good idea to collect lists of words on the computer – current class/group words, words connected with certain sounds. These can be saved as a word-processor file, and displayed on the IWB for short reinforcement activities, such as reading from the screen, covering/revealing, sorting mixtures of words into phonic groups.

3 Spelling lists (word level work) years 1–6

The previous activity leads naturally into collecting and modelling spelling lists. Once lists of relevant words have been collected on the computer, you can use the IWB to set up hide-and-reveal games. Sections of words may be covered up or partially revealed by the 'spotlight' tool, as the children predict the word.

As text is typed on the screen, the usual spell checker feedback will appear, possibly a wavy red line or other highlight. This can be a good occasion to teach and model the correct use of a computer spell checker. It will not give a single right answer, but the user has to display and choose alternative words. Be aware of words which are not picked up by spell checker – homophones, proper nouns, and so on. Where appropriate, teach children how to add these new words and proper names to the spell checker dictionary.

4 E-versions of reading scheme (word level work) years 1–3

When a reading scheme is used, CD-Rom versions can add useful support. Text can be read together on the IWB. The Oxford Reading Tree is a good example, and comes in the form of CD-Roms and a website, Oxford Reading Tree Online.

5 Flowchart software (sentence level) years 2–3

Flowchart software (Kidspiration, 2Create) is a very powerful use of IWB. The teacher can model the organisation and planning of a text. See Chapter 8 (Creative possibilities with ICT) for a fuller account of this software.

6 Keyboard punctuation (sentence level) years 2–3

When teaching punctuation it is important to demonstrate and teach how to find correct punctuation and speech marks on the keyboard as well as in handwriting.

7 Text bank (text level) years 2–3

Scan or type text extracts and save in a class or school resource bank. The IWB is invaluable for shared/guided reading and should be used as part of the daily routine.

8 Concept maps as writing frames (text level) years 2–3

Together with a class or group, you can model story planning or collect ideas using 2Create or flowchart software such as Kidspiration or Inspiration, collecting ideas and immediately placing them together on the board. There is a more detailed account of these programs in Chapter 8. Display the text for discussion as it develops. The texts produced may be automatically presented as a word-processor writing frame/outline which can be copied to each computer to form the basis of individual writing – on-screen or printed on paper.

9 Electronic dictionaries (text level) years 2–3

There are many online and CD-Rom dictionaries – for example, My First Dictionary (Dorling Kindersley). Start to introduce simple electronic encyclopaedias for individual and whole class use. If possible, these should be available on the school network rather than using a disk which can get scratched or dirty.

10 Information finding (text level) years 2–3

The teacher can model finding information from non-fiction texts. Include simple electronic searching – finding words in a text, finding items on a web page, finding information on the internet. Introduce internet searching and how it relates to this. If you want to find a particular word in a lengthy text, an easy way is to use 'Find on this page' on the edit menu of your web browser.

11 Note-taking (text level) years 2–3

Model note-taking with IWB – one child can make visible notes as another child reads a passage. Discuss strategies in practice.

12 Text structure (text level) years 4–6

Model the use of DTP in creating a newspaper layout. You can use the outline mode and document map features of a word-processor to show the structure of long texts. Paragraphs can be rearranged easily.

Essential ICT literacy activities

In this section we list some essential ICT activities to support the teaching of literacy. These are also grouped according to word, sentence or text level and appropriate year group.

1 Dictionaries (word level work) reception, year 1

An electronic dictionary which is routinely available on the computers used by the children can provide a useful additional support for early learning. One well-established example is My First Dictionary (Dorling Kindersley). With this a child can look up words on the CD-Rom from a well-designed alphabet menu. When the word is found the computer reads out a definition in a clear voice.

2 Clicker (word level work) reception, years 1–3

Using a computer QWERTY keyboard is always a challenge. Clicker word banks enable children to start composing sentences without the use of a keyboard. Clicking a word or sentence in a grid displayed on the screen places it in the word-processor. Clicking the right-hand mouse button makes the word speak, helping the child to choose the correct word. As new words are gathered into personal collections, new Clicker grids can be created to support writing, so that a class resource bank builds up.

In years 2 and 3 use Clicker grids and Textease Word-banks for additional support. Clicker grids can be used to build up shared collections of words – which in turn offer differentiated support for SEN. If you have a network this can be a whole school initiative. Children can also build up personal dictionaries as their own files – as a Clicker grid or word-processor document. One cell in a Clicker grid can 'call up' another grid, so complex linked structures of word banks are easy to set up. The 'a' cell, for example may call up a set of words beginning with 'a'.

3 Spelling software (word level work) reception, years 1–3

A number of useful Spelling Practice programs are available, for example, StarSpell, My Spelling Friend. Good spelling software can be easily set up with words which are being explored currently in the classroom, and practises and models the look – cover – write – check routines established by the teacher.

It is important to check that your spelling software allows you to enter and customise lists of words you actually want to reinforce. Starspell (Fisher-Marriott) is a well-established and comprehensive package. It can incorporate relevant and targeted lists of words, reinforcing them with sound strategies. For a free but power-ful resource, take a look at Look, Cover, Write, Check from the Ambleside School site.

To extend support for spelling in years 4–6, further spelling practice software can also include the following packages:

Spellmate (Sherston) – teem review:
http://www.teem.org.uk/findresource/element?element_id=1498&session_id=s_
5&topic_id=

'I love spelling' (Dorling Kindersley) – teem review:
http://www.teem.org.uk/findresource/element?element_id=1293&session_id=s_
5&topic_id=

Wordshark. (White Space Ltd) teem review:
http://www.teem.org.uk/findresource/element?element_id=1702&session_id=s_
5&topic_id=

4 Talking word-processors (word level work) reception, years 1–3

Clicker and Textease are good examples of talking word-processors. Research evidence suggests that speech feedback is effective in helping early writers. As soon as a word is typed, the computer speaks it out, or can be configured to say letter sounds, letter names or blends. Hearing a sentence read back as soon as you type a full stop can be an immediate encouragement to reflect and recheck the sentence.

5 Clicker (sentence level) reception, year 1

Use Clicker word banks to compose sentences without the use of a keyboard, or to add complex words into a text without having to spell them independently. It is very effective to use Clicker 'sentence' grids where the use of a full stop calls up another sentence. This reinforces the importance of using a full stop at the end of a sentence.

6 Text-disclosure (sentence level) reception, years 1–6

Start to use simple text-disclosure/missing-word activities, for example, Developing Tray (2Simple), Sherlock (Topologika). These provide a highly motivating context for word prediction within a sentence. A text – this may be part of a book the class are reading together, a poem, song or information passage – is presented on screen with words or letters missing, so that a group of children has to predict and 'develop' the text. This activity engages all the language cues which a reader uses to decode text – semantic, graphophonic, syntactic, and so on. In years 2 and 3 continue to use extracts from current class reading.

In years 4–6 poetry work, it may be useful to set up text-disclosure activities with nonsense verse – this highlights which words can be easily replaced by others and which are understandable because of context.

7 Tape recorders (sentence level) reception, years 1–3

The tape recorder – a slightly neglected ICT device – can be used to record stories, plays and performances. Headphones are useful in a busy classroom. A headphone 'splitter' is a cheap and useful piece of equipment which allows two children to listen to a tape at the same time. Recording is an aid to purposeful storytelling, for example, making a programme for younger children – it allows insight and reflection on reading.

8 Podd (sentence level) reception, years 1–3

Explore verbs with Podd (Indigo Learning). Podd is a cartoon figure – as a child completes the sentence 'Podd can...' by typing a verb, the character attempts to carry out the action, giving rise to a lot of useful talk about verbs.

9 Writing frames (text level) reception, year 1

Rhyme and pattern writing frame or Clicker grid can be used for this activity. Set up simple writing frames within Clicker or Textease based on predictable rhyming texts. This could be as simple as removing the rhyming words from a poem, or on the other hand, leaving the rhyming words and removing the rest of the text. The resulting texts can be used to give structure to the children's own writing.

10 Text bank (text level) reception, years 1–6

As different texts are used, be sure to keep copies of them on the school network. They can provide a useful basis for a class anthology of story extracts, poems and other texts which can be used again and again to print and/or display on screen/IWB.

As poems are used, add them to this class text database. In a word-processor, collect opening sentences from stories in text resource bank – these are useful story starters.

11 Desktop Publishing (text level) reception years

There are many opportunities for making captions, picture story books and 'big books' with a simple DTP program, for example, Textease, MS Publisher, 2Create. As well as the usual clip art, it can be much more interesting and purposeful to use a digital camera and add pictures to text. In this way children can build up story books or carry out simple tasks such as making picture cards to label familiar objects. With Textease it is very easy to create labels around a picture. Pixel is a software package aimed at the simple creation of labels. You can also use desktop publishing to organise and create class anthologies, posters, wall-display captions with text and pictures.

12 Story planning (text level) reception, years 1–6

A class story can be retold using 2Create. Different children could create story 'cards' with some text and pictures for each event. These can then be linked together in order to make a more sophisticated presentation.

In years 2 and 3, use Kidspiration to make flow charts and plan stories. Develop these class starter plans as writing frames for individual or group use. Use word-processing for planning and early stages of sustained stories. Use Kidspiration or 2Create for children to organise their first ideas, print out and use as a basis for handwritten work.

From year 4 onwards, use a word-processor or storyboard software for mapping out stories and preparing playscripts. These may be continued in handwritten forms. The ICT is most useful at the planning or design stage.

As a writing frame for story development, you can provide text starting points on a word-processor for new scenes to be added. Use Inspiration (flow chart or concept map software) to map out a current story.

Look at the characteristics of stories in different media, especially by using video clips of films. Some are now available online from the BBC Creative Archive.

13 On-screen dictionaries (text level) reception, year 1

Discuss how these ICT sources differ from traditional book dictionaries. In years 2–3 start to use a variety of online and CD-Rom dictionaries – My First Dictionary; simple encyclopaedias – for group and individual reference.

14 Information skills (text level) years 2–3

Use reference CD-Roms and compare the way they are used with written text. Introduce a CD-Rom children's encyclopaedia. This will lead to further work on searching – within documents and on the web. Use cyberhunts – a set of questions which can be answered by visiting a number of different websites. There is a good collection of these on http://www.btinternet.com/~tony.poulter

15 Reviews (text level) years 2–3

As books and poems are read by the children, make a collection of reviews using 2Review. Add non-fiction texts to the class review collection. This will gradually become a very valuable resource for all kinds of work – exploring genres and themes.

From year 4 onwards the ViewPoint/PinPoint Storysearch database (Longman Logotron) is particularly powerful for looking at themes in reading and making comparisons, as it is based on a very thought-provoking questionnaire (see Figure 7.1).

Sort the class collection of electronic texts into fiction and non-fiction. Make a class database of books from the library using 2Investigate, sort in different ways including fiction/non-fiction.

16 Fiction (text level) years 4–6

Use the internet to find author and book information: full details in Chapter 6. From the internet, collect different versions of the same story to compare.

Web links:

http://www.pitt.edu/~dash/type0124.html – five versions of the story of the 'Three Little Pigs'.

http://www.pitt.edu/~dash/grimm.html – Grimm's Fairy Tales

http://www.acs.ucalgary.ca/~dkbrown/storfolk.html – folklore, myth and legend: this has links to: http://www.usmenglish.com/fairytales/cinderella/cinderella.html – The Cinderella Project

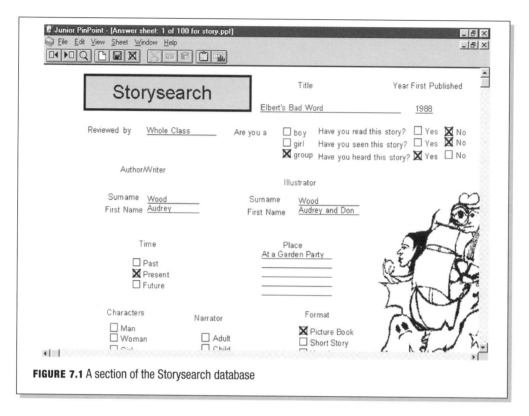

FIGURE 7.1 A section of the Storysearch database

http://www.usmenglish.com/fairytales/lrrh/lrrhhome.htm – The Little Red Riding Hood Project

http://usmenglish.com/fairytales/jack/jackhome.html – The Jack and the Beanstalk and Jack the Giant-Killer Project

17 Word-processing (sentence level) reception, years 1–3

Simple word-processing or DTP (for example, Textease) can be used daily for short writing tasks. The software uses speech to give feedback.

In years 2 and 3 use a word-processor to set up text transformation exercises in short passages, for example, giving a page from a current story, change tense of verbs, substitute verbs, change singular to plural, nouns to pronouns, add punctuation, speech bubbles, and so on. These can be carried out as group or individual activities, and may be printed out for marking.

In years 4–6 extracts of text may be selected and transformed into what is, essentially, a writing frame for further work. Extracts from current stories may be retold from different points of view by transforming word-processed text. Text of all kinds can be redrafted by word-processing to re-express it 'in own words'. Editing text to fit space can provide useful exercises in précis and summary. Use word-processor layout tools effectively for letter writing.

Continue to use word-processing for as many writing tasks as possible, especially for the initial stages of drafting. Sometimes it can be effective to use ICT for the planning stage, even if the actual writing is done by hand.

18 Proof-reading (sentence level) reception, years 1–3

It is useful to set up proof-reading activities with a word-processor, using short sections of children's own writing. The concept of proof-reading – not 'marking' or finding fault, but using computer tools as a support – can help children to revisit a text and prepare it for 'publication'. It engages a group of children practically with many of the key issues of spelling, grammar and punctuation.

19 Drop-down menus (sentence level) reception, years 4–6

It is possible to set up word-processor exercises or writing frames using drop-down menus to allow children to choose alternative constructions. These can be story starters or exercises about particular language elements. See Chapter 8 for a fuller account of how to set these up.

20 Transformations (sentence level) reception, years 4–6

Continue to use the word-processor for transforming extracts of texts, as well as for collecting lists of new words and storing them on the school network. Many language features can be explored using jumbled texts – to be sorted (by dragging and dropping sentences) into the right order. It is also useful for a group to edit a relatively complex text to simplify it for younger children to read.

21 Word-processing activities (text level) years 2–3

Use a word processor wherever possible. Provide differentiated support for children by using Clicker grids and a talking word-processor (Clicker, Textease).

Many text-level transformations are easy to set up, for example, transforming a short extract from a story from third person to first person on a word-processor.

Use the facility to automatically sort text into alphabetical order in a word-processor (in Word, under the Table menu).

22 Writing frames (text level) years 2–3

Writing frames can be set up on a word-processor. These can include Clicker grids with time frames (for example, sentence beginnings for different points in the day); and Clicker grids with simple poetry structures (for example, lines to rhyme, starting and finishing lines, sets of rhyming words).

More elaborate story starters can provide story settings in a word-processor, as well as on-screen writing frame templates for writing character profiles. These may consist of a list of questions to answer about the character, which may be deleted once they have been answered. In looking at character in fiction texts, offer an extract of the story text on part of the screen, and the child can compose a character portrait in the other part (for example, using Clicker grid, text-boxes).

Any poem can be made into a writing frame or Clicker grid for restructuring and extending activities, by removing words and sections. 'Sandwich poems' is a way of extending text (see Chapter 8). Use on-screen extracts to start writing sequels or prequels to a story.

As a source of immediate and motivating ideas, try the story starts available on the Sutton school website.

There are useful writing frame templates available from 'Writing Frames in Word' (Kent). To create your own templates, see the technical section at the end of Chapter 8.

Create writing frames or cloze activities from humorous verses. Starters of a few lines can use drop-down menu choices in Word.

23 Poetic form (text level) years 2–3

In a word-processor, the children are given a poem presented as prose (for example, no line breaks) and are asked to try to organise it into a suitable layout. Discuss the results and give reasons, comparing with alternative layouts.

24 Playscript (text level) years 2–3

As a group activity, transform a story text into a playscript on a word-processor, preferably for a 'real' purpose, for example, producing a play to perform from a current story.

25 Instructions (text level) years 2–3

Sequencing instruction activities may be set up easily with Clicker or any word-processor ('put these instructions in order'). Write instructions for simple use of ICT equipment, for example, digital camera, tape recorder. Create instruction cards for familiar ICT equipment.

26 Note taking (text level) years 2–3

Introduce electronic techniques which can enhance note taking – for example, deleting unwanted text; highlighting key words in another colour. As a word-processing activity, a passage of information text can be reduced to key points by highlighting and deletion.

27 Letters and email (text level) years 2–3

Extend work on writing letters to include the use of email. Use the 'virtual email' software, 2Email, for safe in-house email experience. Children can practise all the skills of handling email in sending messages around the school network in a safe environment.

28 Poetry (text level) years 4–6

In writing poetry, word-processing allows children to experiment with poetic form and revision in a way that handwriting does not. Be sure to save successive drafts.

Prepare poetry texts to present them to the class, highlighting and annotating features using colours, text boxes, and so on.

Use DTP to compile a class anthology of poems. Copy/paste text from children's work or internet sources.

29 Extended writing (text level) years 4–6

Use ICT tools to plan and structure extended writing. Use Inspiration for planning, MS Word outline view and document map.

It is possible to collaborate on extended writing by compiling individual texts into one larger story – using 2Create, Word, PowerPoint, and so on.

30 Newspapers (text level) years 4–6

Creating a class or school newspaper works well with a DTP program – Textease or MS Publisher. Divide the children into publishing roles – reporter, editor, proof-reader, illustrator. For information on real-time newspaper days, see Chapter 8. Explore journalism on the internet by visiting newspaper and broadcasting sites.

Media texts – newspapers, reports, and so on, on the web can be a useful source of first-hand information. When discussing advertising, use video clips of TV adverts as well as printed text.

Use presentation software, for example, PowerPoint, to show key points to an audience, and IWB to show to class.

31 Recounts and reports (text level) years 4–6

Text Detectives (Sherston) offers seven focused activities for this area. Reading Zone is another package with structured activities for this unit.

32 Searching and web skills (text level) years 4–6

Develop internet 'literacy' – the ability to search, find and evaluate information quickly and effectively – within documents and on the web. This involves under-standing search engines – their power and limits. Further development will include key words, 'Reading' websites, as well as exploring CD-Rom adventures and non-linear texts. Develop search skills for e-texts: key words, accuracy, AND, NOT, OR. Explore strategies for taking notes from web sources. Children should learn how to keep a word-processing document open while on the internet, switching applications, copying and pasting relevant material – including the web address line. This should always incorporate work on the validity and reliability of web information.

Simple cyberhunts – questions to be answered by visiting websites – encourage scanning and skimming. There is a good collection of these on http://www.btinternet.com/~tony.poulter/

33 Book information from internet (text level) years 2–3

Use selected websites to find out information about books and their authors from the internet. See resource list.

Extension ICT Use

In this section we list some additional ICT activities which will add extra value to the teaching of literacy. These are also grouped according to word, sentence or text level and appropriate year group.

1 Alphabet software (word level) reception, year 1

There is a wide range of alphabet reinforcement games available, usually in some kind of simple and lively format. A few examples:

ABC-CD (Sherston – Teem review at http://www.teem.org.uk/findresource/element?element_id=1408&session_id=s_5&topic_id=), Alphabet Soup (Compact Multimedia)

Little animals (BBC – http://www.bbc.co.uk/schools/laac/menu.shtml)

BBC Words and Pictures (Sherston CD, BBC website – http://www.bbc.co.uk/education/wordsandpictures/)

2 Practice software – reception, year 1

There are many software packages designed to practise and reinforce aspects of language. They are usually in a game format, and whether you wish to use them is largely a matter of teaching style and taste. Literacy Bank and Literacy Box (Granada) offer a wide range of 'drill and practice' exercises throughout the primary school. At this stage, children should begin to use the computer thesaurus and dictionary as an extension and occasional alternative to printed sources.

3 ICT language (word level) years 4–6

Explore the particular technical language of ICT. There are many acronyms: CD (compact disc), CD-Rom (compact disc – read-only memory), LCD (liquid crystal display), modem (modulator/demodulator), GPS (global positioning system), DVD (digital video disc), blog (web-log) and so on.

Use the internet as a source for obtaining lists of proverbs and finding examples of language change. Many web sites have a useful element of language play, for example anagram generators, sites which create 'Shakespearean insults' and so on.

4 Autoshapes – years 2–3

Introduce the use of 'auto shapes' in a word-processor (particularly Microsoft Word). These can add levels of meaning to a written text with labels, speech bubbles, thought bubbles and stars.

5 Internet texts – years 2–3

When considering non-fiction texts, the internet is a valuable source of material for investigations. Most local newspaper text is available online for news-related studies. It is easy to find examples of pre-twentieth century and other archaic texts which can usefully be explored for language features. 'How stuff works' and similar websites provide a great deal of child-friendly information text.

6 Digital camera – reception, year 1

Use a digital camera for children to collect pictures of text in the environment – road signs, notices, labels, warnings – and display on screen or IWB.

7 Video animations – reception, year 1

Re-enact stories for video – for example, Digital Blue. Using Digital Blue, children can use puppets or toys to tell a story, moving each one very slightly between each frame to create simple 'step animation' and recording the results.

8 Resources for stories – reception, year 1

Children's literature is well-supported on the web – see the full resource list. Useful sites for appropriate stories include Children's Story Books Online, Education Place Tales and My First Reading Adventure: I want to read. To explore folk tales and fables, visit the Fable, Myth, Fairy Stories site. Kent NGfL provide a number of non-fiction on-screen big books, centred around Sebastian the Swan.

9 Fiction – years 4–6

Stig of the Dump – literacy activity collection based on a story.

Find further information about books and authors from the internet, including extracts of work.

Texts for older literature are often freely available on the internet for a variety of activities. Bring older text into Microsoft Word – explore words identified as suspect by spell checker.

Use the internet to collect stories from other cultures, for example, Fables, Myths and Fairy Stories; Anthology E-Books; Mythstories, Bigmyth.

Interschool email projects provide real motivating audience for 'published' texts – as well as school websites. Extend with 'book rap' or an email project around a book.

Literacy World Interactive website.

10 Information handling – reception, year 1

Use simple database software: PicturePoint, 2Graph, to link literacy and mathematical information handling – non-chronological reports, lists, pages, charts.

11 Poetry bank – years 2–3

As a poem is discussed or presented, keep a copy on the network or in a class folder; then, making anthologies from this pool is easy. Add to this pool of stories and poems with texts collected from the internet. The Giggle Poetry site is recommended. It will become an invaluable resource. Use Google desktop search for instant retrieval of texts on any subject or to bring up lists of texts on a particular theme.

12 Poetry – years 4–6

Explore imagery in a poem by making a presentation (for example, PowerPoint slides) using pictures, colours, illustrations for each phrase.

The Poetry Society: (PoetryClass has an excellent range of lesson plans – many of them by well-known poets – links, resources and ideas for teaching poetry).

13 Prepare for story telling – years 2–3

For a storytelling activity, a group of children are given text on screen to restructure and prepare for telling – marking different voices, sound effects, expression instructions and so on. Use sound or video recording to prepare a performance of a poem or story.

Retell stories for audio or video recording; narrate stories for step animation using Digital Blue. Create a step-animated puppet play from script and Digital Blue video.

Use storyboard software, for example, 2Create, PowerPoint to retell main points of a story.

14 Storytelling – years 4–6

From Cornwall, the Brave Tales CD-Rom is an excellent resource for all storytelling activities. It shows video clips of a storyteller in action and has a wealth of material on presentation, cue cards and performance – with traditional Cornish tales to try out.

15 Playscripts – years 2–3

Use tape recording – sound/video to capture and reflect on plays which children have performed. Use the excellent Young Writers' Toolkit (Granada) to write and record scripts for radio plays and other multimedia projects. You will not need any expensive equipment for this, only a computer and a microphone.

Use 2Create or Kar2ouche to present characters expressing their views in thought or speech bubbles.

Use Bigmyth (bigmyth.com) as a resource for retelling myths from around the world (animations with sounds) and also the Fables, Myths and Fairy Stories site and the Mythstories Museum site.

16 Alphabetical sorting – years 2–3

Explore the alphabetical sorting facility on a word-processor or a simple database. For a simple but effective network activity, use a database in 2Investigate. Each member of the class creates a new card and puts a word and picture on it. Each new card appears on each child's computer, and they can then watch the computer sort them into alphabetical order in slow motion. Try with sets of words on different subjects.

17 Instructions – years 2–3

Read instructions for simple use of ICT equipment, for example, digital camera, tape recorder. Look at instruction manuals for familiar ICT equipment, for example, digital camera, tape recorder, 'instructions to make a cup of tea' web activity.

From the internet, use the AA or RAC route-finder to obtain directions or find details of destinations from Streetmap.co.uk or Multimap by typing in postcodes. Compare these sources of information with printed resources.

18 Presentations – years 2–3

Create presentations of material in other curricular subjects using PowerPoint or Textease Presenter. Presentations may also be created in the form of web pages. The simplest way to do this is to save a document which has been created in a desktop publishing program as a web page – the software will convert it automatically. Web pages may be viewed on disk or on the school network – they don't necessarily need to be published for the world to see.

19 Persuasive writing – years 4–6

For a source of material giving supporting evidence on issues and dilemmas from the web, try this RE link – 'Globalgang' (the Christian Aid 'issues' site). There are many sources of official language – for example, government documents on the web. The internet is a vast source of different texts with different biases.

Promethean provide individual handsets so that children can register a vote or answer immediately – the totals appear on the screen. Use this voting technology to assess the persuasiveness of arguments in an instant poll.

ICT can be helpful in creating adverts. For a jingle, use a tape recorder or music software. Photo Story will make a professional presentation of pictures and allows you to construct or insert appropriate music. 2Animate may be used for simple animated sequences in adverts.

Assessment: literacy and ICT

This section will look at the issues involved in assessing children's work in English or literacy in which ICT plays a significant part. In order to assess what learning is actually taking place, it is important to tease out and separate the literacy elements from the ICT elements as far as possible. Obviously, in a literacy hour the main focus is literacy – and that is what we want to assess. At the same time, ICT is increasingly a subject which is embedded in the curriculum. It is often most effective when it supports other subjects, rather than being a discrete area in its own right. If there is an occasion where it is appropriate to assess a child's achievements in both ICT and English at the same time, then that is obviously economical in time and effort for the teacher.

First of all, there are several important issues to be explored.

Common ground between ICT and English

The C in ICT is highly significant. When computers were first introduced into schools, the new subject IT (information technology) was often seen as a study of computers and their applications – software, programming, 'what this machine can do'. The focus of ICT (information and communication technology) is subtly different. It includes the material of IT, but now gives a much greater priority to communication: 'what we can do with the machine'. This reflects a society in which new technology is most used for communication. It is likely that children's most common experiences of ICT outside school will be in the area of communication – mobile phones, stereos and MP3 players, DVD, the internet, email and so on.

One immediate implication of all this is that a convergence is taking place between ICT literacy and general literacy. All the things we expect of a literate child – ability to decode texts, ability to communicate in different forms and genres to different audiences, and so on – are equally true of ICT literacy. It is just that the ICT literate child (or adult) is competent and confident in using ICT as the medium for these communications.

This is reflected to some extent in the curriculum. The following table pulls out some of the ICT level descriptors to level 5, some extracts from the curriculum on the subject of word-processing, and some of the level descriptors for English in the area of writing. Looking at this material some common themes are quite obvious. The level statements for writing (in the English curriculum) and those for ICT overlap and enrich each other.

Level 1: children communicate meaning through simple writing, and using ICT.

Level 2: children communicate meaning and develop ideas – they use ICT to do this purposefully.

Level 3: as their writing becomes more developed and organised, so they use ICT to develop ideas.

Level 4: they are able to use ICT to combine information from different sources with increasing awareness of audience. Their writing also becomes more developed – complex and organised.

Level 5: children make choices about style, fitness for purpose and audience. They begin to reflect critically on their writing.

It becomes clear that a good ICT lesson or piece of work will often exemplify good 'literacy' practice as well. The objectives are the same. The converse will also be increasingly true – a good 'literacy' lesson will now take account of the different modes of communication, including those within ICT.

Level descriptions in ICT and English (writing)

TABLE 7.1 Level descriptions in ICT and English (writing)

ICT	Word-processing	Writing (English)
Level 1 – using ICT to explore options and make choices to communicate meaning. Pupils develop familiarity with simple ICT tools.	… explore information from different sources, showing they know that information exists in different forms. … use ICT to work with text, images and sound.	Pupils' writing communicates meaning through simple words and phrases. In their reading or their writing, pupils begin to show awareness of how full stops are used …
Level 2 – purposeful use of ICT to achieve specific outcomes.	… enter, save and retrieve their work. … use ICT to help them generate, amend and record their work and share their ideas in different forms, including text, tables, images and sound.	Pupils' writing communicates meaning in both narrative and non-narrative forms, using appropriate and interesting vocabulary, and showing some awareness of the reader. Ideas are developed in a sequence of sentences, sometimes demarcated by capital letters and full stops …

TABLE 7.1 Level descriptions in ICT and English (writing) (continued)

ICT	Word-processing	Writing (English)
Level 3 – using ICT to develop ideas and solve problems.	...use ICT to generate, develop, organise and present their work.	Pupils' writing is often organised, imaginative and clear. The main features of different forms of writing are used appropriately, beginning to be adapted to different readers. Sequences of sentences extend ideas logically and words are chosen for variety and interest. The basic grammatical structure of sentences is usually correct. Spelling is usually accurate, including that of common, polysyllabic words. Punctuation to mark sentences: full stops, capital letters and question marks is used accurately...
Level 4 – the ability to combine and refine information from various sources. Pupils interpret and question the plausibility of information.	...add to, amend and combine different forms of information from a variety of sources. ...use ICT to present information in different forms and show they are aware of intended audience and the need for quality in their presentations. ...exchange information and ideas with others in a variety of ways, including email.	Pupils' writing in a range of forms is lively and thoughtful. Ideas are often sustained and developed in interesting ways and organised appropriately for the purpose of the reader. Vocabulary choices are often adventurous and words are used for effect. Pupils are beginning to use grammatically complex sentences, extending meaning. Spelling, including that of polysyllabic words that conform to regular patterns, is generally accurate. Full stops, capital letters and question marks are used correctly, and pupils are beginning to use punctuation within the sentence...
Level 5 – combining the use of ICT tools within the overall structure of an ICT solution. Pupils critically evaluate the fitness for purpose of work as it progresses. – increased integration and efficiency in the use of ICT tools. A greater range and complexity of information is considered.	...use ICT to structure, refine and present information in different forms and styles for specific purposes and audiences. ...exchange information and ideas with others in a variety of ways, including email. ...assess the use of ICT in their work and are able to reflect critically in order to make improvements in subsequent work.	Pupils' writing is varied and interesting, conveying meaning clearly in a range of forms for different readers, using a more formal style where appropriate. Vocabulary choices are imaginative and words are used precisely. Simple and complex sentences are organised into paragraphs. Words with complex regular patterns are usually spelt correctly. A range of punctuation, including commas, apostrophes and inverted commas, is usually used accurately...

The 'masking' effect of ICT

Using a word-processor or desktop publishing program, it is possible to create publications which look very professional – in their standard of print, illustration and layout. Work created with the help of ICT often looks much more sophisticated than work created by hand. This is very useful in creating presentable or publishable work for an audience, but can be highly misleading in assessment. For example:

A child completes a piece of writing using Microsoft Word. Every time he starts a sentence, the word-processor automatically inserts a capital letter with autocorrect, even though he does not know about the rule himself. A teacher may choose to turn this feature off, so that she is able to make a realistic assessment of the child's ability.

The spell-checker in a word processor alerts a child to spelling mistakes as soon as they occur. She corrects each one from the list of options. The teacher can find no evidence of the child's spelling strategies by looking at her text.

Using a Microsoft Publisher 'wizard' a child produces a very impressive Christmas card, with illustrations, titles and greeting. It prints correctly, enabling a single sheet to be folded into a card, an operation which requires some text to be printed upside-down. This apparently 'high-level' task has been done by simple clicks and choices within the wizard, and actually reflects very little thought or skill at all.

A child presents a bundle of information material she has collected from the internet for a class project. She is unable to read most of it.

These examples show how easy it is to 'over assess' work created using ICT. In many schools, there are still some teachers who feel less confident than their children in the use of new technology. It is very easy for these teachers to be impressed by children's work when they exhibit skills which seem very advanced to the teacher. In this case the actual achievement of the children may be seriously over-estimated.

In the early years of ICT in school there were many sheets for assessment which focused on technical aspects and skills. Obviously, skills are important and need to be assessed, but these sheets only scratch the surface of ICT assessment. The ICT literate child or adult will develop towards a literacy which operates at high levels of comprehension and reflection. If the child's writing on a word-processor is assessed according to the English curriculum statements, these will present quite a close correlation with the ICT statements, and should take priority in this area of communication.

Process and product

The printed outcomes of an ICT activity – because of these factors – can present a very inadequate and misleading picture of a child's ability. It is vital, at every stage of education, to be able to capture process – and not just product – before we can assess the quality of learning. Here are a few everyday practices which can help to make process explicit.

Saving drafts

Working on a piece of extended writing on a word-processor, encourage children to save drafts at regular intervals during the writing process. Using 'save as...' a story about an island is saved as island1, island2, and so on. This means that process is recorded. Material from early drafts may be retrieved and used again in a re-design of the story, and a map of the process of composition is available to the teacher. This is a practice used by 'real' authors.

Commentary

It can be very useful to occasionally ask children to describe the process they have gone through in creating an ICT text. This can be a spoken or written commentary – and it provides an occasion for reflection as well as providing high-quality information for assessment. 'Thinking about thinking' – or meta-cognition – is taking place here. An ICT journal is a possible context for this. A display of 'published' 'fair copy' work will be much richer if it includes such a commentary about drafting stages and skills.

Recording activities

ICT provides many devices which can record activities as they occur in the classroom or on a field trip. Digital cameras, video, sound recording devices such as dictating machines – all these can capture elements of process in a class project, and support the recount or telling of the project.

Modelling writing

Using an interactive whiteboard can be a powerful way to make process explicit. A displayed text can be marked up and redrafted with a class of children using the electronic marker pens and all the tools of the word-processor.

Display

All display which incorporates printouts, or other ICT outcomes, should also include text or images which place them in a meaningful context and reveal something of the processes involved.

Assessment resources for ICT

Level examples

The government's exemplification site for the national curriculum: National Curriculum in Action – www.ncaction.org.uk – is an excellent resource for levelling and assessment of children's work. For almost every subject of the curriculum, it offers examples of work which are levelled appropriately for the age and ability of the child. Each example has a full commentary. It is possible to collect portfolios which relate to the range of ability in the class you teach.

Progression

The following comments on progression markers in English, are adapted from material available at http://www.ncaction.org.uk/subjects/english/progress.htm.

In speaking and listening, progression is characterised first of all by confidence and competence in adapting talk. In the ICT context, this means making the most of occasions where ICT is a catalyst for talk. Progress is measured by the increased skill and flexibility of pupils in communication. Progression in listening with understanding will involve perceptive responses and concentration. Participation in discussions will be encouraged by effective use of ICT.

In reading, progression is characterised by engaging with increasingly demanding texts, using a repertoire of reading strategies. ICT plays a significant role in this, and children's response to text disclosure programs can give very precise assessment information. 'Pupils' confidence in understanding texts that are more challenging' will also include ICT texts. Good use of ICT will involve a great deal of 'responding, ... analysing and evaluating' texts. Here, as is often the case, good ICT is also good literacy.

'Reading for information' is a central ICT/literacy strand which parallels ICT progression precisely: 'Pupils progress from locating information for a specific purpose ... to collecting and synthesising it for different purposes ... and then putting such material to further use'.

In writing, progression is characterised by developing skills in writing, and increasing control of different forms of written texts. The notions of purpose and audience become increasingly important – ICT provides many useful activities in which progress in this area can be assessed. Electronic presentation is a very public and motivating mode in which pupils can show their 'ability to adapt writing for meaning and effect'.

There are often a number of children who are particularly adept at ICT – often able to perform operations which many teachers would find baffling. This can mask the assessment information for literacy. A document about recording, assessing and levelling work in English by the more able child can be found at http://www.qca.org.uk/12560_1079.html. This document advises gathering a range of assessment data before concluding that a child is particularly able. Here, once more, high achievement in ICT and literacy both show similar characteristics – increasing complexity and effectiveness of communication. The levelling schemata provided here by QCA do not take ICT media into account – it will be necessary to do so if a realistic assessment of an able child is to be achieved.

Assessment in ICT

Formative assessment (or assessment for learning) happens as pupils record their work and reflect on it, as teacher (or computer program) give feedback. Summative or teacher assessment of learning is carried out at the end of a unit or year or key stage. It is based on level descriptions. ICT is so much embedded in the curriculum, that most assessment is formative. It needs to be quite nuanced, taking care to look at process far more than product. The teacher will always be looking for evidence of change in the pupils – change in attitudes, confidence and response – and it is important to build into planning ways of recording these changes. These can include profiles (described below), keeping ICT journals to encourage reflection, and frequent brief opportunities for children to write or talk about what they are doing with ICT. These issues are developed a little further in a 'Lighthouse for Education' document (http://www.thelighthouseforeducation.co.uk/ict/assessingict/assessingictks1and2.htm), which places ICT assessment very clearly in a wider context and gives practical examples of formative and summative assessments.

Student profiles

A set of documents from Becta (http://curriculum.becta.org.uk/docserver.php?docid=340) provides a workable and coherent strategy for assessing ICT work using student profiles. This can easily be adapted to record ICT achievements within learning about literacy. There are examples of several different profiles, at different levels, including the teachers' notes. According to BECTa:

> It is important…that a regular note is made showing the date, some indication of the context being used and the evidence that has been witnessed. These notes should be made over a period of the year (or key stage) and should be supplemented occasionally with examples of the child's work.

It is suggested that these notes are 'coded' according to the ICT content of the activity:

TABLE 7.2 Coding assessment notes

Exchanging and sharing information	E
Finding things out	F
Developing ideas and making things happen	D
Reviewing, modifying and evaluating work as it progresses	R
Breadth of study – using ICT inside and outside school	B

Inevitably, many of these will appear frequently in literacy activities. Here is an extract from one of the example profiles (Winston, working around level 4):

---

21 September
Winston used the word-processor to redraft the notes he made on life in his grandparents' time (E). He said it was lucky that he could use his notes which he had saved before, otherwise he would have to start all over again (R).

21–22 September
Winston and his friends set up an experiment to monitor changes in temperature in different locations in the school grounds over a period of time. They printed out and displayed their results (D).

24 September
Winston used the painting package to create images of his grandpa and grandma. He played with different colours and screen effects before deciding on his final choice (E).

22–25 September
Winston used the music program to recreate the skipping rhymes which his grandmother used to sing. He recorded them onto the tape recorder, adding percussion instruments to his computer-generated sounds (D).

Over a period of time, these notes build up a picture of the level at which the child is working, as well as showing up any areas which are not being addressed in that child's experience. Record-keeping like this meshes well with ongoing self-assessment by the child. A log of ICT activities maintained by the child can record use of the computer and other ICT equipment. It could take a journal form in which each page was as follows:

TABLE 7.3 Log of ICT activities

Date	Activity	ICT used – e.g. software	What can I do that I couldn't do before?

At the very least, this offers the teacher a sense of how much engagement with ICT is actually taking place.

Teacher's ICT journal

Many teachers still find the implementation of ICT to be quite a problematic area. As a personal staff development tool, it can be extremely useful to keep your own ICT journal. This can include the following.

Diary

Keep notes, random jottings, annotations on ICT activities you have been involved with:

- On your work at home, on the course, and in school with children – state the context.
- Display the processes of your learning, not just the outcomes. Be reflective.
- Record clearly the steps you take when engaging with new work: record to remember.
- Record the good and bad aspects of your experiences.

Problem solving

Identify your problem – particularly in the areas of ICT and literacy – take action, find a solution.

- Record 'what you don't know': state your problem clearly.
- Use this record as an aide-mémoire for action.
- Identify a person, program or text that will provide the information you need. Resolve your problem: find a solution.

Collections

Remember that, in ICT, the most useful information is this week's information:

- Clippings and quotes on ICT gathered from magazines, newspapers, and so on.
- Relevant information discovered on the internet.
- Information about the use of CD-Roms.
- Information on subject teaching and learning in schools.
- Print-outs of children's work.
- School ICT policy documents.

Own work in ICT

Instances of pedagogy:

- Worksheets and materials you have made using ICT.
- Annotated print-outs of children's ICT work.

- How you have used software in the curriculum: be critical

Children's ICT activities

- Notes on what children have done. Give the content, age group, how they responded, what worked, what didn't.
- Record children's common mistakes.
- Children's ICT journals: are they keeping them? How are they using them?
- Listen to children's conversation as they use the computer. Note significant processes and responses.

Classroom management issues

- How did you manage the learning?
- What are the possibilities and limitations of ICT in your classroom?
- Identify strengths and weaknesses in managing individuals, groups, whole class.
- Management of resources.
- How many children can work at the computer effectively?

This will build up into a powerful resource for reflection and personal development.

Future developments

It is notoriously difficult to assess ICT and literacy together, as the process and understanding are always more important than the products and outcomes. New technologies provide interesting possibilities of recording process, through web-cams, keystroke recording and 'intelligent' software.

Worcestershire LEA has developed the Managed Assessment Portfolio System (MAPS) in collaboration with TAG Learning. This enables pupils to develop their own electronic portfolios. Teachers can use these examples to develop a school portfolio, which can be moderated across the LEA. Pupils work online, and they are able to upload drafts of their work, including annotations and interactions, to capture process. More details at www.maps-ict.com.

QCA have funded an assessment project at Ultralab called eVIVA, which provides an innovative way of assessing the ICT capabilities of students. Students compile online portfolios to show what they know and can do, the processes they have used, and the decisions they have made. eVIVA embraces websites; electronic messaging; mobile phones and SMS. Once students have completed their portfolio, they have a unique telephone assessment – their Viva – which they can take on their mobile phone. More details at: www.eviva.tv

New technologies will undoubtedly make the process of assessment more precise and powerful, which, in the long run, can only enhance good planning and effective learning.

Web links

http://freespace.virgin.net/sound.houses – Andrew Rudd's website

http://www.camelsdale.w-sussex.sch.uk/teach_with_ict2.asp – Camelsdale First School

http://www.teem.org.uk/findresource/element?element_id=1535&session_id=s_5&topic_id – Oxford Reading Tree Teem review

http://www.amblesideprimary.com/ambleweb/lookcover/lookcover.html – Look, Cover, Write, Check spelling software from Ambleside School site

http://www.teem.org.uk/findresource/element?element_id=1498&session_id=s_5&topic_id – Spellmate (Sherston) – Teem review

http://www.teem.org.uk/findresource/element?element_id=1293&session_id=s_5&topic_id – 'I love spelling' (Dorling Kindersley) – Teem review

http://www.teem.org.uk/findresource/element?element_id=1702&session_id=s_5&topic_id – Wordshark (White Space Ltd) Teem review

http://www.btinternet.com/~tony.poulter – Cyberhunts

References

Bennett, R. (2004) *Using ICT in Primary English Teaching*. Exeter: Learning Matters.

Gamble, N. and Easingwood, N. (eds) (2000) *ICT and Literacy: Information and Communications Technology, Media, Reading and Writing*. London and New York: Continuum.

Goodman, S., Lillis, T., Maybin, J., and Mercer, N. (eds) (2003) *Language, Literacy and Education: A Reader*. Stoke-on-Trent: Trentham/The Open University.

Leask, M. (ed.) (2001) *Issues in Teaching using ICT*. London and New York: RoutledgeFalmer.

Loveless, A. and Dore, B. (2002) *ICT in the Primary School*. Buckingham: Open University Press.

Loveless, A. (2003) *The Role of ICT*. London, New York: Continuum.

MacFarlane, A. (ed.) (1997) *Information Technology and Authentic Learning*. London and New York: RoutledgeFalmer.

Monteith, M. (ed.) (2002) *Teaching Primary Literacy with ICT*. Buckingham: Open University Press.

Wheeler, S. (ed.) (2005) *Transforming Primary ICT*. Exeter: Learning Matters.

8

Creative possibilities with ICT

Chapter overview

This chapter describes a range of materials and ideas which can promote creativity in the primary school, particularly in the area of literacy. These include mind mapping for text design, using digital camera and video, using presentation, multimedia, web design and word-processing software in many new creative ways.

Introduction

In this section we will look at a number of items of hardware and software which encourage creative use of ICT in literacy teaching. Stephen Heppell has written about the way in which computers are marketed for productivity when what education requires is creativity. In the arts and media, computers are an indispensable part of all kinds of design processes. A musician will often record songs onto a computer, where they become available for detailed editing. Notes can be removed, or transposed. Instrument sounds can be transformed and the tempo can be adjusted. Artists and designers use ICT in the same way. A picture may be cropped, edited, adjusted in colour, electronically collaged, and so on, before it goes to print. The computer has become a 'space' in which all kinds of creative possibilities can be made real, and even if I am not very good at the techniques of music writing or drawing, the computer enables me to use my creativity at a higher level.

These 'real-world' activities provide a model for educational ICT. How can we use the computer, especially in the area of literacy, as a creative space? How can it help children release and develop their innate talents? We continue with some practical accounts of specific items of software and hardware, suggesting ways in which these can release creativity in children's literacy development. The list is indicative rather than exhaustive. Priority is given to affordable equipment and easily available software, as well as new uses for materials which most schools will already possess.

Mind map or concept map software (for example, Inspiration)

'Inspiration' is a software package which enables the user to create concept maps or flowcharts. Planning written work is a priority of literacy teaching, and Inspiration is a particularly powerful tool for this process. You click on the program screen and an ellipse appears, in which you can type a word or phrase which can be the central or starting idea. Other words in balloons can be added anywhere on the screen, and can be assigned different shapes, colours or pictures. The ideas can be linked with arrows to form a flowchart. If 'rapid fire' is chosen, a series of words may be typed quickly, and will form themselves into a spider's web of links. You can add a 'note' to any of the points or 'nodes' on the screen – a comment, or a paragraph pasted in from another text. In this way a structure of thought may be built up.

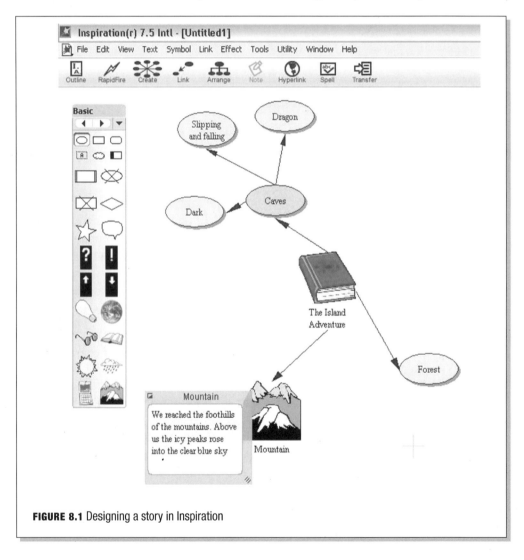

FIGURE 8.1 Designing a story in Inspiration